Angels
See Through
Eagles' Eyes

In Loving Memory of

Dad and Mom,
Bill and Martha Ellis,
for showing me how to
care, share, laugh, and love.

Grandma and Grandpa Ellis
for showing me true faith and
trust in God and unconditional
LOVE.

Rebecca Clover
for being an Earth Angel
and touching my heart,
and so many others.

Larry Green
for being the ultimate
friend and support system
for anyone blessed to meet him.

Karrie Hanson
for lighting up the world with
her smile, enthusiasm, and
dedication to family and friends.

Dr. David Penner
for being the wind beneath my
wings with unwavering support
of nonsmokers' rights.
We made a difference.

TABLE OF CONTENTS

ACKNOWLEDGMENTS

Thanks to the angels who encouraged me—Jean-Noel Bassior, Don and Carol Honstain, Geri Larkin, Carol Morency, Mary Manin Morrissey, Judy and Ned Powell, Irma Conrad Turko, and Dinesh and Chandra Vora.

Thanks to the angels who supported my dreams—Mitchell Artis, Barbra Bloch, Pam Carls, Barb Delozier, Laura Dombrowski, Jim and Terry Donnelly, Margaret Doran, Shawne Duperon, Mike and Corliss Eden, Rev. Joy Fletcher, Kam Flynn, Bob and Sally Frakes, Ann Galloway, Karen Green, Helen Halpin, B.J. and Ken Harper, Melissa Hellman, Fadi and Mirna Issa, Laura Jaffe, Terrie Knox, Kat Knudsen, Joe Kubek, Carolyn Morgan, Mary Parker, Richard Patton, Elaine Pitman, Nancie Rosenberg, E.J. and Carol Sands, Nancy Sarti, Evelyn Scafuri, Bob and Kathy Serlin, Jeff Shafe, Nancy and Louis Sokol, Ed and Georgia Stachura, Marian Umpfenbach, Anne Marie VanDuyn, Barbara VanGorder, Tina Vassalo, Harry White, June Williams, Faye Wills, and Candi Zimmerman.

Thanks to the angels who inspired me—Rev. Karen Boland, Nancy Briggin, Gladys Cherrett, Alan Cohen, Sue Dahlmann, Gail Doherty, Diane Dorcey, Dr. Wayne Dyer, Jimmy Ellis, Katherine Fischer, Linda Hanniford, Craig Hanton, Paula

ANGELS SEE THROUGH EAGLES' EYES

Harker, Kristen Hartnagel, Mary Juarez, Rev. Annette Jones, Rev. Edward Jones, Patrice Karst, Maria Kaupp, Rev. Ortheia Barnes Kennerly, Reid and Jennifer McLellan, Karyn Myers, Joe Meo, Kaye and Edwarda O'Bara, Mary Lou Palazzolo, Beverly Pepin, Dr. Robert Purdy, Marci Rule, Dr. Robert Schuller, Annie Sciacca, Julie Smith, Gordon and Jo Sparks, Denise Squires, Davanne Stahlbusch, Jim Tuman, Oprah Winfrey, Maureen Wotton and Ashley.

Thanks to the angel of verse—Margo LaGattuta for introducing me to the world of words with a bag of stones and shells.

Thanks to the energy and music angels—Donna Eden and Robert Gass for introducing my mind to new energy techniques and sounds.

Thanks to the angels who expanded my horizon—Lee Carroll, Steve Conrad, Jim Ellis, Danny Hahn, Garry Hermeston, Linda Kent, Bob Koenders, Gordon Libby, Linda McCandless, Marilyn Ellis Mileham, Robert Richards, Sensei Anthony Sanchez, Jan Tober, and Rosalia Wilson.

Extra special thanks, gratitude and total appreciation to the two angels who helped me through the good times and bad—Julie Geyer and Leslie Miles. I wish everyone could be blessed with good friends like you two.

Blessings and gratitude to my angels at AboutBooks, Inc., for helping me get these words out to the world—Marilyn Ross, Cathy Bowman, Sue Collier, and Kate Deubert. God sent Deb Loeser and Classic Printers to answer my prayer to get this book out by Christmas 2001. Thank you, Deb for being my angel.

Listen to the Silence

Listen to the silence,
Deep inside your head,
Voices, music, free advice,
In the safety of your bed.

Listen to the silence,
The words will come, you know,
With peace and understanding,
And advice before unknown.

Listen to the silence,
The music and the rhyme,
The inner soul is talking,
About memories of time.

Listen to the silence,
Deep within your soul,
Be aware of peace and calm,
And love to make you whole.

Listen to the silence,
God is talking through your guides,
Telling you to trust yourself,
True happiness lives inside.

Jane Ellis Conrad, August 16, 1994

TO THE READER

---·◆·---

Have you ever heard voices in your head and thought you were going crazy? I have, too.

Quiet Voices began drifting through my head after my paternal grandfather died in 1955 when I was ten years old. They were soft and friendly, like playmates in my head who comforted me when I was lonely or someone had hurt my feelings. When they came, I pushed them aside. I could never tell anyone about them. Only crazy people heard voices. I had nightmares about men in white coats putting me in a straitjacket while I was sleeping and carting me off to the "funny farm." Imagine how scary it felt to think about being whisked away from my family and locked in a padded cell just because I heard voices others didn't.

The Voices were my secret for thirty-five years, until cancer threatened my life in 1990. My surgeon told me the cancer had been growing at least two years and had probably invaded my liver and bones. Only two choices came to mind: clean out my closets or pray. I prayed. *Dear God, if you want me to go, I'll go. But if you let me live, I'll do anything you want me to do. Go wherever you want me to go and touch whoever you send my way. My life is in your hands.*

Once I surrendered to God, faith replaced doubt and wonderful coincidences started happening. The Voices started coming daily with direction and purpose. Facing death made life more meaningful. I have a deeper appreciation for friendships, laughter, and love—a clearer vision of my goals and purpose on earth. I know all about pain and sorrow, but I choose to focus on the moments of ecstasy and joy.

I'm just one of many people walking the earth who are divinely directed by these Voices. You may know us, or we may be strangers who just show up when you're in need. We're God's messengers called Earth Angels. The two things most Earth Angels have in common are faith in God and a head-on collision with death. Sometimes it's an accident or a health challenge that left the decision to live or die in God's hands.

This book is about my journey—what I hear, where I go, and what I do. When the Voices come, I take action. The people I meet may need inspiring words, a healing touch, or just someone to listen.

Today is my arena. Yesterday was my classroom. Tomorrow is where my dreams reside. Right now is where I live.

Each day I get up and say, "Thank you, God, for another day." Then I cram as much as humanly possible into all my waking hours. At night I fall into bed and say, "Thank you, God, for this day. Please give me one more."

How's *your* life? If it's less than perfect, you might want to start listening to the small voice inside of you that may be directing you to endless possibilities. Are you open and receptive to having angels in your life? They may be calling your number but getting a busy signal. Just open your lines of communication and get call-waiting. Believe me, this is one call you won't want to miss.

When I opened my heart to God, the fog cleared and angels appeared. Angels appear to those who believe. And believing is seeing without using your eyes.

Missions

My goal is not to teach or preach
But just to be me.
Then others will see life
Through the eyes of a child
And the wonderment
That lies within.

Jane Ellis Conrad, April 12, 1994

Mission of
an Earth Angel

How powerful is prayer...really? Powerful enough to commute my death sentence.

In January 1990, the surgeon told me that cancer had been growing inside me for at least two years and had probably spread to my liver and bones. I prayed after hearing that news, and God must have heard my prayers. Upon further exploration, the surgeon discovered the cancer was contained in the ducts and hadn't spread as he predicted. He was stunned. I was thankful to God.

After the surgery I needed six months of chemotherapy to eliminate any renegade cancer cells that might cause future problems. Instead of having the chemo drugs injected in my arms, I opted to have an Infusaport surgically implanted in my chest. The surgeon made it sound like no big deal. Ninety percent of the time he was able to insert it on the first try.

A needle was used to freeze the tissue where the cut was made, then he fished a long tube down the incision into my chest. He hit some unfrozen nerves. I moaned. After eight more tries, I started coughing up blood. I felt as if I'd been run through with a hot poker. The pain was horrible, and I let out an agonizing cry. He had punctured my lung. He said he couldn't figure out my anatomy and would have to stop.

"You've got to finish it so I can take chemo!" I insisted. He checked his watch and agreed to try three more times. I prayed that God would guide his hands and let it happen. On the third try, the line connected to my blood source, and he hurried off to his meeting.

Once the doctor was out of sight, my emotions exploded. I sobbed uncontrollably while the nurse held me in her arms. After my sobbing and shaking subsided, she wheeled me to the X-ray department to assess the damage. When she moved my right arm above my shoulder to get a clear picture of my collapsed lung, excruciating pain shot through me. But it was only a taste of what was to come.

Over the next few months I used my mind to control the pain. And there was lots of it. When I touched my right ear, pain shot through my chest. I stopped touching my ear. My dog, Miss Mattie, was a great distraction and a source of comfort when I needed someone to console me. When I felt as if my chest was caving in, Miss Mattie would look into my eyes and lick my face. She said so much without uttering a word.

I wish my husband of twenty-two years had given me as much attention. During the surgery I lost more than tissue— I also lost the physical closeness of my mate. He became more self-centered and aloof. I kept a smile on my face to mask the heartache from his rejection. In some ways, my cancer became his albatross. He was more scared of my death than I was. Was living really better than dying if my marriage disintegrated? Several years later he apologized for not having been more supportive, but by then it was too little, too late. My mind had already shielded my heart from further rejection. That was the beginning of the end of the marriage. I survived, but the marriage died.

God and I had the cancer under control so I was close-minded when well-meaning people tried to tell me about faith and coping with illness. I didn't want to read the books they

Carjacking

As my friend Amy and I drove along 16 Mile Road on that bright, sunny Saturday afternoon, I thought we were just on our way to the Comedy Club for dinner and some laughs. Then I saw the clean-cut young man jump out of the back seat of the car in front of us. His movement snapped me out of a daydream. I noticed the anger in his eyes as he scanned his surroundings. Then he slid back into his seat and closed the door.

The Voices came: "Pay attention. Something big is going to happen."

His car bumped the car in front of it. An elderly, heavyset woman got out of her car to assess the damage. There was no reason to be fearful. After all, she was in a middle-class neighborhood, on a busy street, in daylight, surrounded by other vehicles. Right? Wrong! Before she could get back in her car, the man with the angry eyes jumped out of his car, ran, and grabbed her from behind.

"What's he doing to her?" my friend blurted out.

"It doesn't look like anything very friendly," I said in amazement. Suddenly the Voices kicked in with great urgency, "Honk your horn now or she will die!" Without thinking, I laid on the horn. I kept honking until the light turned green and the man returned to his car. He looked around, just like before.

Amy shrieked, "Get out of here! He's got a gun!" I saw him shove the steel-gray handgun into his jacket pocket, as he slid into the back seat of his car, which quickly made a sharp U-turn, cut through traffic, and headed in the opposite direction.

7

I called 911 on my cellular phone and relayed the criminals' and victim's physical descriptions, vehicle makes, models, and license numbers to the police, and agreed to answer more questions at the station. Amy was too upset to go with me. In fact, when I dropped her off at the Comedy Club, she reamed me out. "It's stupid to go to the police! These criminals have no regard for life! They'll kill you! Let the victim testify. You did your duty by calling in."

The tables had turned. I felt that instead of being supported for helping someone in need, I was a victim, too. Why was she yelling at me? Hadn't I just been divinely directed to save that woman's life?

I ignored her warning and headed for the police station. There I learned that state and local police had joined forces to find four criminals who had stolen at least five cars from a local mall. I supplied the few missing pieces that completed the puzzle. The carjacker's fate was sealed when they turned in front of a police car that had just received my carjacking information.

As I entered the front door of the police station, the handcuffed carjackers were brought in through the back. One of the detectives commended me for honking my horn because it had distracted the criminal and drawn attention to the situation. He told me that the carjackers had been squealing on each other and weren't interested in harming the witnesses.

He also verified that the elderly woman would have been killed if I had not intervened. The punk with the gun wanted to "pop" someone—kill a complete stranger for no reason at all—that day. Then he told me that her seven-year-old granddaughter had been in the front seat of the car screaming in terror.

These two innocent victims probably never knew that they'd had an angel experience. Would they have died on that beautiful sunny afternoon if I hadn't been there to honk my horn? Or would someone else have been sent to rescue them?

The Voices came: "Good job. We know you can be trusted to listen to and act on our messages, so you'll be given more responsibility. Your new title is Master Jane, Earth Angel."

I was thankful for a lot of things that day—for the Voices directing me to help the victim be safe, for my cellular phone, for the officers' quick response, and for the clear view I had of the event. I was also glad my horn worked that day—because it had stopped honking six weeks earlier.

Stone of Endless Possibilities

The reaction is usually the same when I lay the clear, colored bead of glass in the stranger's reluctantly outstretched hand. It could be light blue, dark blue, or green depending on which color Spirit wants them to have. As they look at it and feel its energy, I say, "Do you know what this is?" Their answers are either, "No," "A worry stone," or no guess at all.

Then I hand them a small, clear, plastic bag with my business card(s) and a bright pink card that reads: "STONE OF ENDLESS POSSIBILITIES. Hold this stone and know in your heart that whatever you dream, believe, and put action to, you can achieve. You are LIMITLESS."

That's it. My mission is complete. I give, they receive. They can do whatever they want with it. Keep it. Throw it away. Or give it away. There are thousands of stones floating around the country and soon the world.

What impact will a small glass stone, a bright pink card, and a few loving words of encouragement have on the world?

STONE of Endless Possibilities

Hold this stone and know in your heart that whatever you dream, believe, and put action to, you can achieve. You are LIMITLESS.

Achievement Networking Team   810-978-8582
2899 E. Big Beaver, #306   FAX: 810-978-9089
Troy, MI 48083-2466   earthangel@unidial.com

If it unlocks one person's door to their endless possibilities, I've done my job.

From time to time people call to say, "I'm holding your stone and wanted to say you've made a difference in my life." I say, "It's just a reminder that you're right and perfect and have no limits. Bless your heart for giving me feedback. *Namaste.*" I like to say *Namaste,* which means "the light in me sees and honors the light in you." When you say "bless your heart," you get a brick. With the bricks you build your mansion in heaven and on earth.

One day I received a call from a man I met in Baltimore at the "Whole Life Expo." He was in a panic. "You have to send me more stones. I was in a car with some friends on the beltway in Washington, D.C. Our car was spinning out of control and I thought we would all die. I grabbed your stone from my pocket and said a prayer. At that moment, our car glanced off the median and stopped. There was no damage to the car or any of us. Your stone went flying. I never found it. You have to send me more stones."

I know it was the prayer that saved him. The stone was just the visual reminder of his belief in the only one who could control the outcome…God.

Another time I received a thank-you call the day after giving a stone to a new acquaintance at church. She was an inner-city kindergarten teacher.

While walking to the school parking lot with the principal at night, they were robbed at gunpoint. When the criminal grabbed her purse and ran, her wallet fell on the ground with the bright pink card and stone landing on top of it. Her purse was taken but thankfully not her life.

------◆◆●◆◆------

Car Crash

The car crash happened just minutes before I arrived at the post office. The front end of one car had steam rising from the hood. A police officer was bent over the driver.

"Pull your car into the post office parking lot and assist the injured driver," the Voice commanded. As I approached the car, the officer moved away to let me in. The Indian woman was delirious yet trying to get out of the car. "You'll be okay, just stay in the car. EMS is on the way," I said. Then I started doing Reiki to her head and chest. That calmed her down. There was trauma to her face. She mumbled that her jaw was dislocated.

The police officer asked her if he could look in her purse. She nodded approval. He opened her wallet and said, "Are you a doctor?"

I thought he was talking to me so I replied, "No, I was just driving by and stopped to help."

"Not you," he retorted. She was a doctor at a local hospital. What an honor, I thought. I was sent to work on a doctor.

I briefly chatted with the police officer who told me some of the injuries he has seen as a result of air bags blowing up and causing some serious injuries to the head, neck, chest, and back. This doctor's jaw had been dislocated due to the force of the bag. I realized then that air bags may save lives, but I think they should be an optional feature in cars.

When EMS arrived, I moved away. On the way back to my car I laughed to myself. I'm supposed to blend in—not be highly visible. To arrive unexpected and leave undetected. This time I was wearing an orange outfit that made me stand out, and a badge with my name and my company's name that took away my anonymity. It's not important for anyone to know my name, just the fact that there are people on earth God sends in time of need. We're called Earth Angels.

Reminder of Dad

I saw a man in the parking lot that reminded me of my dad. I debated whether or not to give him a Stone of Endless Possibilities. Should I or shouldn't I, my head debated. Then my heart spoke, "How could you not do a small Random Act of Kindness that might make a big difference in the life of this frail older man who is someone else's dad?" I know my dad would have been touched if a stranger did a kind gesture for him.

I slowly approached him and in a little girl's voice, which came from who-knows-where, I said, "Excuse me, sir. You remind me of my father. May I give you this?" And I gently slipped the cobalt blue stone into his slightly opened hand along with a bright pink card that said "Stone of Endless Possibilities."

I never looked back. I just turned and slowly, pensively walked to my van, and slid behind the wheel. As I drove through the parking lot toward home, tears rolled down my cheeks. Along with my next breath came a sorrowful sigh. In five days, Dad will have been gone five years—Friday, May 5, 1995, to Friday, May 5, 2000. He loved life and often took people out for dinner, ordered a cake, and sang "Happy Birthday," even when it wasn't their birthday. On May 5, 2000, I'm having a few friends for dinner, buying a cake, lighting five candles, and singing for Dad. He would have liked that.

A Pilot, a Priest, and an Angel

Sometimes my trips take many turns before my actual assignments begin. On the way back to Detroit from a business trip in Portland, Oregon, my connecting flight to Seattle was delayed, so I missed my direct flight home. I was put on the next flight, which had a stop in Minneapolis.

The flight seemed routine until the pilot announced that the Minneapolis airport was fogged in, our plane was low on fuel, and the crew was almost to the end of their allowed flying time. He would make one pass at the airport but might have to fly on to Fargo, North Dakota, for fuel, which is what happened. (I really didn't need to know about the low fuel part.)

Once we arrived in Fargo, there was no replacement crew or fuel to take us back to Minneapolis. So the plane was emptied and passengers shuttled to various hotels in the area. I found a convenience store a block from the hotel and bought contact lens solution and other toiletries. It was 2:30 A.M. We were given free transportation, lodging, breakfast, and returned to the airport about six hours later.

I'm not usually concerned about being rerouted or delayed because there is always a reason why I'm somewhere other than where I think I'm supposed to be. My next two assignments began in Minneapolis.

I usually sit next to elderly people in case they need assistance. My next assignment was an immaculately dressed woman in her seventies with beautiful white hair. She was on the way to Detroit for her granddaughter's wedding. We chatted for a while, then heard the announcement that our scheduled flight to Detroit had engine trouble. We had five minutes to make our way three gates away to the next departing plane for home. Since she had heart problems, I told her to walk at a normal pace and I would run ahead and let the airline folks know she was on her way.

Once she was in her seat and baggage stowed, I made my way down the aisle to the next vacant seat. It was no surprise that I ended up in the emergency aisle next to the door. That's where I usually sit because I know in case of an emergency the angels will help me open the door and assist people down the slide.

Sitting one seat away from me in the aisle seat was a pilot in full uniform except for his hat. He was reading a car magazine and minding his own business. The last of the passengers were in their seats. Charging up the aisle came my second assignment.

He also was in full uniform minus the hat. But he flew for God's airline, just like me. He was a priest. And not a very happy one at that. After stowing his case in the overhead compartment, he looked at the pilot and said, "Are you a pilot?" My silent Voice kicked in, "No he's Bozo the Clown. Of course, he's a pilot. Can't you see?" For the next minute, which seemed like ten minutes, the priest unloaded all his negative baggage about the airline on this poor unsuspecting pilot. From inconvenience to incompetency and everything in between. He was definitely having a snit fit and not being very nice.

I asked Spirit for guidance. After he settled his substantial frame into the seat, I said, "Isn't this ironic? We have a pilot, a priest, and an angel." His body jolted. The plane took off.

"Do you want to hear some stories?" I asked. Before he could answer, I told him my carjacking story and one other. I also told him there are only two things people need to remember in order to have peace in their lives—forgiveness and love. That did it. He grabbed his magazine and was very well behaved for the remainder of the trip. I'm sure the pilot appreciated his change in energy also.

As we approached Metropolitan Airport, the priest said, "I'm so late, I don't know how my driver will find me." To which I replied, "No problem. I'd be happy to drive you home." His body jolted like I had hit him with paddles, and he sputtered, "No, that's okay. He'll find me."

The wheels touched down. When the plane came to rest and the door opened for departure, the priest quickly stood up, opened the overhead compartment, and grabbed his case. As he was bringing it down to traveling level, he looked at me and pondered, "Forgiveness and love. Forgiveness and love." Then he turned and shuffled down the aisle. The pilot and I looked at each other and smiled. No words were exchanged yet we both knew a life had been touched with a few precious words.

<hr />

Why Are the Children Dying?

Her name was Kayla. A name whispered by children with sweet innocent voices that were breaking up with emotions. Faces stained with tears. Too young to lose a friend through violence. A name murmured by adults and children around the world.

What made her different? She was six years old, lived in my home state of Michigan, and was shot dead by another six-year-old in her classroom. Why?

How life has changed since I was in first grade almost fifty years ago. My most traumatic experience was someone hitting me or hurting my feelings. Instead of lashing out, I'd go to the corner of the playground and suck my thumb.

So many victims. So young. Why, God? Two children. Low income, by national standards. Two different races and sexes, which is not the point. What happened in Michigan is a reflection of the violence in the world. The names, faces, locations, and ages have changed.

How many guns are needed? How much violence can kids watch on TV, video games, cartoons, and movies without having it spill out into their everyday world? The children are acting out what they see. How many kids see an actor being killed one week then showing up next week on another show? That is acting, this is life and death.

When someone is killed, they are gone. Dead. Adios. Out of here. It's the last hurrah. Death is final! No show next week. No Bobby Ewing dying on *Dallas* one year then showing up in the shower a few years later and calling it a dream. It's no dream. In death there is no encore, no second chance. The final bye-bye.

If we just support the TV shows and movies that reflect our values, wouldn't the entertainment industry have to change?

Indigo Children—
Problems or Gifts?

I struggled with this chapter because I tried to write it rather than let my heart spill out onto paper. All my life I have struggled to find the me that society calls normal. From as early as I can remember I was different from other kids. It felt better being with older people rather than those my own age. People I could learn from and accept me the way I was. How many people are there in the world who feel like I felt? Struggling, searching for their identity. Alone and not knowing where they fit in. This was my life, like so many others. Very bright. Gifted. Knowing we're okay, just different. Like being outside looking through a window at everyone else and not finding a seat with my name on it. I learned from seeing and hearing rather than reading. More right-brained than left. Back then I would have been classified as an "Indigo child."

I used to play Barry Manilow's song "All the Time" on the piano. What I had "all the time" was a kind and loving heart and sensitive feelings that would often be hurt by insensitive classmates.

Babies, older people, and animals accepted me, but not my peers. When hurt, I went within. That's where my Voices would comfort and console me. But that's not like having someone to go shopping or play ball with. I found myself going from group to group. I'd do something with one group of kids. Then move to the next group, not really belonging anywhere.

I was always very curious but didn't have anyone to sit down and teach me. There was one outstanding teacher, Mrs. Bennett, and two Girl Scout leaders who mentored me. Mrs.

Bennett was my fifth and sixth grade teacher. She sent me birthday cards until I left high school. About twenty years later, I located her and got three former classmates together to take her and her husband out to dinner. We gave her a gold heart necklace because that's what she had—a 24-carat heart. I'm glad we reconnected before she died of cancer.

Grandma Ellis made me feel special, with her tender touch and words of encouragement in a Scottish brogue. She was all love and the best dispenser of truth and wisdom without saying much at all. She just *was*. Love poured out of every inch of her 5-foot frame and every ounce of her being. She was small in stature and giant in wisdom. Grandpa Ellis was the same way, although I don't remember him as well because he transcended when I was ten years old—that's when my mind went blank and the Voices started. Kind, loving, God-filled messages telling me that I was okay. Those Voices got me through my teenage years and through life to become the person I am today. Carrying on the legacy of my grandparents.

Isn't it ironic that my Voices are gifts that give me direction, guidance, comfort, joy, and peace of mind? Others are frightened when they hear voices and push them aside

When I was eleven years old, my parents received two Dymo label makers for Christmas. I examined both of them and noticed the trigger was sticking out a little farther on one than the other. I decided to fix it. As I unscrewed the last screw, the entire label maker erupted into a mass of flying parts. It took the rest of the day to find all the parts and reassemble them with direction from my Voices. I got it back together and in working order, and had parts left over. I thought about sending the extra parts to Dymo but didn't think they would listen to a kid. Maybe they figured it out on their own.

If you know anyone who is very bright yet struggling to fit into society's mold, have them read *The Indigo Children: The New Kids Have Arrived* by Lee Carroll and Jan Tober. When I read this book, the most peaceful feeling washed over me. All these years I had been an Indigo child!

Indigo children are unique and gifted. As high-energy, non-judgmental, extremely sensitive, and intuitive individuals, they are totally in the present reality and have special needs and requirements. What we can do to assist them is to be understanding—to honor, respect, and develop their many gifts. Indigo children require our love and support to create a "Heaven on earth." If we recognize them for who and what they are, they will help us find our truths, our purpose, and our peace.

Now *my* mission is to help others accept themselves for who they are and be at peace. The Indigo children truly are God's gift to the world.

———◆———

A Mother's Love— A Joyful Journey

This journey actually began in the fall of 1996 when I heard Dr. Wayne Dyer give a heartwarming talk at my church about the O'Bara family. Before Edwarda O'Bara slipped into a diabetic coma in 1970 at age sixteen, she said to her mother, Kaye, "Promise you won't leave me, will you, Mommy?" Kaye replied, "Of course not. I would never leave you, darling. I promise. And a promise is a promise!" Except for ten days she spent in the hospital with a heart attack and some speaking engagements, Kaye has kept her word.

Unbeknownst to me, the O'Bara family was my next assignment.

I was going to write to Dr. Dyer about helping Edwarda (The proceeds from Dr. Dyer's book, *A Promise Is a Promise*, help support Edwarda.) but never quite found the time. Six months later, the pieces of this adventure started falling into place.

In January 1996, God sent me a fantastic network marketing opportunity distributing magnetic energy products. The company's philosophy is based on total health and balance in body, mind, family, society, and finances. The distributors I've met are spiritual and dedicated to helping others. Although I already had three businesses and wasn't looking for another, this one touched my heart because of its products: magnetic sleep pads that put the body into deep delta sleep, shoe inserts that may increase energy and strength, relax pads and bipolar magnets that promote healthy bodies and overall wellbeing by relieving stress and discomfort.

Since my bout with cancer, wellness has been of paramount importance to me. These products restored feeling to my arm, which had been numb for six years, and restored warmth and flexibility to my cold, stiff fingers. When I saw the products and heard heartwarming testimonials from people whose health and lives had been improved, I knew in my heart this opportunity had been sent from God.

In February 1997, while attending a massage therapy class, I met Susan. She was a lawyer and biochemist who hadn't worked in five years after a car accident left her with a closed-head injury. I told her about the magnets. She saw the vision and became a distributor.

Susan found out that all my sleep systems were on loan to prospective customers so she offered to buy me one for my personal use. I appreciated the offer but felt it was too generous. The Voices interrupted my thoughts: "Ask Susan if she would like to donate the sleep system to Edwarda O'Bara." Susan is a warm, caring person and was very receptive to helping Edwarda. We placed a three-way call to Kaye. She accepted Susan's generous offer of the sleep system and invited us to visit her and Edwarda in Miami. That was Monday afternoon, March 31, 1997. I called four airlines, and wasn't surprised to learn about the high prices and lack of flights to Miami—it was Easter week and all the convenient flights were full.

"Dear God," I prayed, "Susan and I really want to help Kaye and Edwarda. If you want us to go to Miami, please supply the transportation." The reply was *Loud*—*"Who do you think sent you the van?"*

"I'm sorry," I humbly replied. "I love the van. I just thought Miami was a long way to drive in a few days. I'll call Susan and tell her we're driving."

The previous month, while struggling to put a sleep system in the back seat of my compact car, I had said to God, "I really need a van. Any kind of van will do...old, new, mini, conversion...anything you want me to have." Two days later a friend called to tell me she was selling her van.

"Great, I'll buy it."

"Okay," she responded. "I'll finance it for you."

If you want to see a good example of prayer in action, just look at this event. I asked for a van, and two days later it was there. And it wasn't your ordinary, run-of-the-mill van. It was a Chevy Cobra conversion van with a remote-controlled bed, dual stereo system, four seats that recline into beds, shades, and curtains.

"Thank you, God!"

At 11:00 A.M. on Thursday, April 3, 1997, Susan and I finished loading the van and began the first leg of our 3,150 mile, five-day round trip from Detroit to Miami. We intended to drive straight through, but God had other plans.

We turned off I-75 and headed for Asheville, North Carolina, about 10:30 P.M. The van was going about 55 mph when the left rear tire blew. I steered over to the shoulder and called 911 on my cellular phone. We were about five hundred yards from the split in the highway that was marked with big directional signs...left to Asheville...right to Chattanooga. Within two minutes a police car pulled up. The officer had the tire half-changed by the time the dispatched officer arrived. The first officer had been on his way to work when he spotted our shredded tire and stopped to help.

We spent our first night in the Wal-Mart parking lot waiting for the tire department to open at 7:00 A.M. Since Wal-Mart was open twenty-four hours a day, we had access to a restroom, snacks, and a security guard who watched the van throughout the night. We were on the road by 9:00 A.M. with four new tires.

If it hadn't been for this unexpected stop, we would have missed a perfect day to drive through the Smoky and Blue Ridge Mountains—seventy degrees, bright sun, no clouds.

It took about fourteen hours to drive from Knoxville, Tennessee, to North Hollywood, Florida, which is just north of Miami. We stopped at a motel about midnight, but contrary to the vacancy sign out front, there were no vacancies. We used the motel restroom, then pulled to the back of the parking lot and slept in the van.

After spending two nights in the van, we needed to find someplace to clean up. The Voices directed me to drive north toward Boca Raton: "What you need will be on this road." About five miles down the road, we pulled into a park with restrooms and outdoor showers. That might have been the quickest shower I've ever taken. The water felt about forty degrees. The custodian let us use his supply room to plug in our hair dryers and electric curlers.

I was in the final stages of getting ready, with my toiletries spread out on the bathroom counter, when a blonde woman in her early twenties skated in on Roller Blades. While she washed her hands, I told her about our journey plus my magnet business opportunity and products. She lost her job the day before and had skated to the beach to pray for help. I told her it was no coincidence that we met and agreed to call her after our appointment in Miami.

Kaye O'Bara had given us good directions, so we had no trouble finding the ranch-style house protected by a black iron fence. A huge rosebush in the front yard had one main trunk, no thorns, and five different-colored roses on the same bush.

Saturday and Sunday were visiting days, so we met some of the O'Bara's family and friends. Peacefulness blanketed the house. Kaye has taken magnificent care of Edwarda over the years. She feeds her, bathes her, draws blood, gives injections, and turns her every two hours. Edwarda's skin was soft and smooth, and she's never had a bedsore. Her waist-length braided hair was salt-and-pepper gray. Her nightgown was lilac and matched the bedsheets. Kaye and Susan talked to Edwarda, and I chatted with the other visitors. I shared my stories about cancer and other missions I've been given, plus our current journey.

The sleep system had arrived two days before we did. Kaye brought it out of the closet, and Susan and I proceeded to pull out all the components. There was a mat, pillow, quilt, and large magnetic massage roller. Then Kaye spotted the item that got her excited—a handheld plastic case with two silver-colored, spiked bipolar magnetic balls. Kaye had been rolling golf balls on the bottoms of Edwarda's feet and was thrilled to use this new product. When this device was rolled on Edwarda's feet, her toes started to move. Because Kaye only sleeps about two hours at any time, she wanted to try out the sleep system herself to see if it made her sleep and feel better.

Kaye gave us something to eat and some of Wayne Dyer's books and calendars. Wayne calls Kaye every day and just happened to call while we were eating. Susan and I were thrilled to have the opportunity to talk with him. We said our goodbyes and headed for the freeway. What a fantastic experience.

We gassed up the van, bought some juice and snacks, and left Miami at 5:30 P.M. We drove to Hilton Head Island, South Carolina, where we spent the night in a church parking lot. Susan called Kaye in the morning to find out how she felt after using the sleep system.

For twenty-seven years, Kaye had slept on her side in a chair next to Edwarda's bed, never sleeping more than two hours at a time and waking up with numb legs and discomfort in her hip. The sleep system was wide enough that she could turn over and get a deep, restful sleep.

"It was the best sleep I've had in twenty-seven years. An hour and a half on the sleep system was like a four-hour deep sleep. I got up and was full of energy. The discomfort in my hip and leg was gone. I've never given a product endorsement or testimonial in twenty-seven years of being asked, but I'm giving you a testimonial about these great products."

After hearing that good news, Susan and I just looked at each other and smiled. God had put us together to help others. Except for delivering a cutting from a five-colored, thorn-free rosebush to Kaye's friend in Michigan, the rest of the trip home was very uneventful. Our mission had been a success. We didn't bring Edwarda out of her coma—she'll come out when the time is right. Maybe we were just sent to help Kaye. Whatever reason we were sent, it was a fantastic, spiritually uplifting adventure.

Thank you, God. Mission accomplished. I anxiously await Your next call.

If you would like to contribute to the Edwarda O'Bara Fund, please see page 109.

————— •◆• ◆•• —————

Best Assignment

Don was the best assignment I've had so far because he listened to the messages I gave him and took action.

He prayed. I was sent.

It was New Year's Eve, 1998. Don and I were both invited to join mutual friends for dinner, and then a dance at church. Whenever I'm invited somewhere, I go because there is always at least one person I'm to help in some way.

I attended the dinner, but he didn't. After dinner we all drove to church. The energy in the dance room was flat so I went to the chapel to pray. *Dear God, with deep humility, gratitude, love, and joy, I thank you for your love, support, and opportunities to grow and be in service to you and mankind. Thank you for trusting that I'll act on the messages you send. Thank you for the energy and compassion being channeled through me to help people be well physically, spiritually, and emotionally. Whatever you want me to do, I will do. Wherever you want me to be, with whoever, whenever, I will also. Not my will but thine be done. I surrender to your will. I'll be back at midnight because I don't want any strangers kissing me.*

When I wasn't dancing, I sat at a table with friends from dinner or walked around. They kept talking about Don. *Where's Don?* Someone called him. *He's on his way.* About 10:30 P.M. Don appeared and sat next to me.

At 11:45 P.M., I just finished dancing when the DJ announced a Ladies' Choice. I knew my next assignment was about to begin when a force was pushing me from behind right toward Don. I was almost running. He looked surprised as I ran up to him and said, "Do you want to dance?" We laughed about this later, because he said I was flying at him and that's exactly how I felt. He never heard it was a Ladies' Choice and I wondered if he thought I made that up. We danced like Fred Astaire and Ginger Rogers. At midnight the music stopped and everyone around us hugged and kissed to celebrate the New Year. He didn't kiss me. I was impressed. After all, he was a stranger.

Eight people came back to my house after the dance for breakfast and a burning bowl ceremony where we all wrote down anything negative in our lives that we wanted to get rid of. Don took over and coordinated this effort. All the negative papers were put in a bowl, taken outside, and set on fire. The ashes were thrown toward heaven with these words, "God, please take these things that no longer serve a purpose and replace them with only positive things that are for our highest good." Then we all made another list of all the positive things we wanted in our lives. We were instructed to read this positive list morning, noon, and night every day to create peace and harmony in our lives.

The last people were leaving at 4:30 A.M., and Don asked if I needed help cleaning up. Normally I would do it myself, but I thought it was so nice of him to offer so I took him up on it. I invited everyone back to a New Year's Day open house starting at noon.

When Don and I were cleaning up the kitchen, he started talking about the heartaches in his life and what led him to church that night.

He was put in an orphanage at age two and had to fight for everything he had, including underwear. At six he was adopted by loving people. Yet he was angry and beat up his classmates. A wise coach channeled his energy into wrestling and football. At ten, his eye was poked out with a hockey stick. He had been married three times, had two sons, raced cars, had been on drugs and alcohol, and was currently in a ten-year relationship with someone who wanted more from him even though he paid all the bills, did the shopping, cooking and cleaning, and was devoted to her three children.

Don was an excellent pipe fitter and welder in spite of only having one eye. His foot was crushed when a pipe fell on it at work seven months earlier, and he was on disability leave. His girlfriend said she'd rather clean the condo than go to the dance. If he went, she hoped he'd never come back. He'd been looking for a place to live for the past four months when she said she wanted to be by herself and he needed to move. On his way to church, he sobbed and prayed. *God, whatever I did or didn't do, I'm sorry. Please forgive me and send someone to love me unconditionally.* God sent me.

On January 3, after church, Don and I had breakfast with some friends then went back to my house. We talked and he excused himself to go outside to smoke. I asked him if God were to lend him a Rolls Royce at birth and asked for it back at death, would he take care of it or trash it. Your body *is* the Rolls Royce, I told him. He said he had quit smoking sixteen years ago and needed loving support.

Since he was basically homeless, I offered my spare bedroom until he could find a place of his own. Besides, I was going to California in a week and it would help me to have someone in the house to take care of my dog, cat, and businesses.

I lent him a magnetic sleep system and magnets for his shoes and did energy work on him when the nicotine withdrawal made him sick.

Spirit told me to have him get in touch with his adopted mother who he had been estranged from for two-and-a-half years. When he called, they both cried. His father had died the past Thanksgiving and she hadn't known how to reach him.

When I got back from California, he went to the doctor who was astounded to see the improvement in his foot from using the magnets. The doctor took him off disability, stopped physical therapy, and said he could return to work. Don immediately called his union representative and started a new job within a few days. Then he answered an ad in the newspaper and found a beautiful condo to rent.

Within eighteen days of meeting me and acting on the messages I got from Spirit, Don got out of a dysfunctional relationship, was reunited with his mother, quit smoking after sixteen years, got off disability, found a job, and moved into a condo.

It pays to listen.

100th Goose Story

The goose and I began our journey about 5:00 P.M. on Saturday, August 14, 1999, in the middle of a two-lane road winding through Oakland University in Rochester Hills, Michigan.

I was on the way to my friend Terrie's to do some energy work. The goose was flopping around on the road so I pulled my van off on the shoulder and approached it to assess the damage. Its wings were flapping furiously, but the goose was not moving and couldn't take off.

I retrieved a navy blue bedspread from my van and threw it over the goose. It calmed right down. I scooped it up, jumped in the van with the goose on my lap, and headed to Terrie's for help. She agreed to go with me, so we headed for the Humane Society. En route we approached the Auburn Hills

Police Station and decided to stop there instead. I took the wrapped-up goose into the station and told the two female officers of my predicament. While they were calling Animal Control, I uncovered the goose and started petting its head, doing Reiki on its back and wings, and telling it that everything would be okay. The officers looked at me like I was a little crazy for talking to the goose.

Since Animal Control didn't pick up, they sent me a block away to the Oakland University Police Department where they called an independent animal trapper. Again, I uncovered the bird, stroked its head, and did Reiki on its back while one of the officers warned me, "That's a wild animal. It's going to bite you." It didn't look to me like it was going to bite me and I didn't want to get bit, so I removed that thought from my consciousness.

Once the trapper came, he said, "I'd take the goose to the Humane Society, but it's closed." He suggested I take it home until Monday morning. I wrapped up the goose, jumped in the van with the goose on my lap, and headed home. There I put my large dog crate together. In went the goose and bedspread. Then I put in a bowl of dry dog food, raisin bran, and seven-grain bread, and set the crate on a table in the back yard. I opened the door to give the goose more water. It started to hiss and then spotted the oven mitts I had on and decided this was not a good sign, and stopped hissing and never hissed after that.

I called Chandra, a wonderful woman who rescues animals and told her about the goose. She called a veterinarian, and at 10:30 P.M. Terrie and I took the goose to get checked out. The legs weren't broken, but he thought it might be in shock and would be okay in a couple days. He told me to take the goose home. So, back in the van went the goose. I took Terrie home. The goose spent the night in the van, in the crate, with the windows open for fresh air.

On Sunday morning, I checked the goose about 7:00 A.M. It was awake and sitting up. My angels told me to call Saint Francis, who is my friend Craig. He lives on 10 wooded acres with a pond and is a wonderful, kind, compassionate soul who would help me with the goose. I agreed to meet him at church. I called Terrie and said, "The goose and I are going to church. Do you want to go?" On the way to Terrie's, I sang silly goose songs, like...oh, goosey, goosey gander, why did you wander, join your gaggle, gaggle, gaggle, gaggle...and such. The goose seemed to enjoy the music, and I felt we were bonding although I'm sure anyone else would have thought I was a little silly. I love animals. They accept you no matter how goofy humans think you are. They think you're okay.

So I picked up Terrie, stopped for a takeout coffee, and headed for church. We put the goose carrier under the tree and met Craig in church. After church, we reloaded the carrier in the van and drove to Craig's. We took the carrier along the trail to the pond at the back of the property and opened it; but the goose just sat there like a lump, watching us. After about fifteen minutes it started flapping its wings and lifted out of the carrier into the water and weeds. Then it pushed out into the open water where it started to drink and eat. Our eyes locked. We were connected. I wished the goose a safe journey wherever God wanted it to be. He wished me the same.

I think this will be the 100th goose story, just like the 100th monkey story. This goose will tell other geese that not all humans want to harm them. That there are light workers and Earth Angels that will protect and help all God's creatures, big or small, two- or four-legged, just because it's the right thing to do.

I chuckle just thinking about what must have gone through that goose's head. It was minding its own business, found itself in the middle of a street, had a cover thrown over it, was kidnaped, taken to two police stations, put in a dog carrier, taken to a vet where its legs were put through intensive physical therapy and maneuvering, given dog food, raisin bran, bread, and water, spent the night in a conversion van, was serenaded with goose songs, had about ten trips in a van, was taken to church and carried through the woods, had the lid lifted off its confinement, saw people laughing and having a good time waiting for it to jump up and leap into a pond filled with sweet smells, cool water, and bugs to eat. Then to top it off, the one who kidnaped it told it to have a nice journey. Wait until I tell my goose friends about this. They're never going to believe it.

The following week, I went to Craig's house to check on the goose. It stayed for one day and supposedly flew off with a flock.

About six months later, I met Craig's girlfriend at a show. She told me about a lone goose that has been in the neighbor's pond since our goose disappeared. They named it Mason. Isn't that great? There's a goose out there named Mason Conrad.

When my life passes in front of me in heaven, I know this day will make me smile, especially the expression on the goose's beak when he spotted my oven mitts.

Oprah's Angel Network

Two days after retiring from a twenty-four-year marriage, Spirit woke me up: "Today you will be given the master plan for your next five years of life. You are to make ten million dollars."

My eyes popped open. "Wow! Ten million dollars. How in heaven's name am I going to do that?" I asked.

"This assignment will be fourfold. First, you will develop a plaque and award program incorporating angels. Second, write five books. Third, a movie will be made from one of the books. Fourth, take two of your inventions to market."

I asked, "What would I do with all this money?" The reply was, "Set up scholarships. Education is hurting in this country, and it is the key to happiness and ultimately world peace. Smart—peace. Dumb—fighting and war. All people need to be educated."

This message came on Saturday, November 5, 1994, at 8:35 A.M. I wouldn't know the true importance of that date for six months.

The plaque program was developed and the first two were given to my incredibly loving, kind, wonderful Dale Carnegie instructors, Diane Dorcey and Sue Dahlmann, who are truly Earth Angels.

A couple years later, I reviewed the progress of my master plan. I was no where near ten thousand dollars let alone ten million. I asked God what I should do. "Tap into someone with the same cause. The one that has more clout. The vision...the resources...and connections. Join the path with others that know the importance of education."

That's when I found Oprah Winfrey's Angel Network. People from all around the country collect money and send it to the Angel Network. I bought a large plastic baby bottle and put vinyl letters on it: "Oprah's Angel Network...for scholarships." I took the bottle with me whenever I did magnetic massages so people could donate if they felt so compelled. The first bottle of money was turned in at a local mall collection point. I never counted the money. That didn't seem as important as the collection of hearts that participated.

The second bottle of money was sent directly to Oprah. I was in my kitchen when the message came: "Go downstairs and make an angel plaque for Oprah. Right now." I know when the message is that strong and emphatic, I'd better get moving. I turned on the engraver and the words came.

The plaque was black glass with a layer of black brass. An angel sprinkling stars and hearts adorned the upper left corner. "With love and gratitude...Oprah Winfrey...Earth Angel—You cried with us...You laughed with us...You loved us. We are better people for having known you. From all God's children whose lives you've touched."

I was told to send the plaque, bottle of money, and some of my spirit-given writings via UPS second-day air to Oprah at Harpo Productions in Chicago. Two days later I called to find out if the box had arrived. When a woman answered the phone, I said, "I just wanted to let you know that I sent a box to Oprah and it should arrive today." To which she replied, "You can't just send something to Oprah. Someone has to request it. The mail room will probably open the box and return it to you."

"But there's money in the box for the Angel Network," I responded.

"Well, who told you to do that?" she retorted.

"God," I said. There was a brief silence. Then in a very loving, kind voice, she replied, "Well then, I guess it will get to her."

Two weeks later I received a letter from the Angel Network thanking me for the money and one from Oprah's assistant saying, "Ms. Winfrey likes your spirit." I was finally on a TEAM, which means Together Everyone Achieves More. As an Indigo Child, I always felt alone. Now I could add my paint strokes to a bigger canvas.

For information about Oprah's Angel Network, see page 109.

Talents and Gifts

Angels to guide me,
And show me the way,
Peace and contentment,
Spirit soars high.

They show me the way,
To a joyful existence,
My spirit soars high,
And reaches toward heaven.

A joyful existence,
Is there for the asking,
I reach toward heaven,
And find inner peace.

Love is mine for the asking,
Heart's bursting with joy,
Now finding inner peace,
True Happiness beyond belief.

Jane Ellis Conrad, October 2, 1994

The Day I Saw God

My eyes were filled with the most brilliant light I had ever seen, as if someone had thrown open the shutters and I was staring at the sun, only more intense. A mass of beautiful colors, like iridescent silver and gold glitter, swirled around counterclockwise with royal blue in the center. Spinning like a tornado without the funnel. The beauty took my breath away. I asked for guidance. "This is the most beautiful sight I have ever seen. What is it?"

The Voices came: "You have seen God. God is an energy field, and the center of the Universe. Throughout the ages, God has come to earth in human form because people would not have known how to pray to an energy field. The Holy Spirit is God's voice. You have listened to the silence and acted on our directions. The reward for your true faith and pure heart is to see and know God in body, mind, and spirit. Share this knowledge with others. Religion is just a vehicle— God is the destination. Don't think your religion is the best and only one. Respect the rights of all people to find God in their own way whether it is in church sharing the experience with others, or communing with nature in a sweet-smelling forest or beside a cool mountain stream. Religion is exterior— the words. Spirituality is interior—the feelings.

"Love one another. Help one another. Be the best you can be to the glory of God. Be successful and have abundance. Share your abundance with others. Help others maximize their potential. Give people hope, a kind word, a gentle touch, a loving smile. Touch lives with love. Live in peace, Earth Angel. And teach others by your example. Release control and manifest your destiny. You are blessed."

When I meditate, objects and forms appear in white, black, and gray. That day, I saw God's light in color.

Spiritual messages sometime appear as red splotches on my body in the shape of angels' wings, hearts, and even the Christian fish. They are blood-red, like birthmarks, and last up to fifteen minutes.

One morning, after meditating, I went into the bathroom to get ready for an appointment. I took my nightgown off and gasped—on my midriff was a perfectly shaped, bright red Christian fish symbol. It was as big as my hand!

Three more messages appeared that day while I was running errands. As I pulled out of my subdivision, the first car I saw had a Christian fish on the trunk. "Okay, God. What is the real meaning of all these messages?" I asked. The Voices came: "Look to the left." I noticed a beautiful old stone building with a sign that read "William Ellis Company."

"What are you trying to tell me?" I asked.

You see, that was my dad's name. He'd just died a few weeks earlier. But he certainly had not owned that building. I drove two more blocks and saw a sign that read "Horn of Plenty."

"Your dad is okay in heaven and you will be okay, too," the Voices said. I was grateful for this message and felt at peace with his passing.

I stopped by the stone building about three weeks later to share my story with the owner's wife and secretary. As I told my story, their eyes widened. The owner had the same name as my dad: William Henry Ellis. He was a contractor. My dad was an architect. His parents were English and Scottish and had come to the United States through Canada—same as my dad's parents. This man had a son named Jim, same as Dad. The man's son Jim had a daughter named Jane, like me. Coincidence?

I drove by the stone building about a year later. The sign was gone. It had been covering a stone plaque that read "Church of Christ." I drove by the building three months later and the original sign was back up. I wondered if the sign had really been down—or had I somehow looked through it to see that God was in residence with my dad and me?

Recommended reading: *God Made Easy* by Patrice Karst. In a very simple, little book, Patrice joyfully explains the destination (God) and the vehicles (religions). This is a wonderful pocket book for all ages.

Sunbeams

Have you ever had sunbeams stream down from heaven and attach to your car? This is a common occurrence for me when I'm driving. They started connecting to me shortly after my father transcended to heaven.

I was driving to Traverse City, Michigan, with my friend, Barb, to attend a trade show. I can't remember ever seeing such a variety of clouds before. There were big puffy white clouds; angry, black jagged clouds; wispy, feathery clouds; multiple layers of clouds with a trace of robin's egg blue in the distance.

My dad was the topic of conversation when the clouds parted and a laser beam of bright white light came from the sun and attached to the left bumper of my car. We both gasped and sat in stunned silence for a few minutes. I said, "Maybe this is a sign from God that we are to ask for our hearts' desires." So we started saying our gimmees...gimmee a house, a car, a trip—material things. But in our hearts we both knew that these were not what really mattered. When the gimmees started, the clouds covered the sun and the sunbeam was gone.

We looked at each other and knew our focus needed to switch to gratitude. "I'm sorry, dear God, for asking for more material possessions when I should be thanking you for your grace. Thank you for our safe journey. Thank you for the opportunity to serve you by helping others. Thank you for our friendship." The gratitude continued for ten minutes or more. When they started, the clouds parted. Two sunbeams attached to the car. One on the left side by me, the other in the middle by Barb.

Since that time, sunbeams have been with me when I travel. They are a great source of comfort and security. There have been up to three attached at the same time. If the sun is out, one will attach to my left bumper. Often a second sunbeam will attach to the middle of the windshield, and sometimes a third one is in between the other two, pointed directly at my heart.

Next time the sun is out, check to see if a sunbeam is gracing you with its warmth. It may just be a loved one calling from heaven to let you know all is well. Or maybe it is God shining down on you with unconditional love and acceptance. Telling you that you're right on course to fulfill your heart's desires. And showing you the way.

Who Am I?

Quite often I get messages for other people. If they have never heard messages themselves, they usually ask me the same questions. "How do you *do* that? You hear voices and act on what they tell you? How long have you been hearing? Is it scary? What messages do you have for me? Why can't I hear?"

I believe anyone can get messages if they talk to God, then just close their mouth, open their ears, and *listen*.

The Voices are not what I do. They are who *I am*, the God within my heart. When the Voices come, I go. I don't know where or why. I don't even know where I'll end up. I just respond.

I've been hearing since I was ten years old. My mind is blank except when I'm getting messages or consciously calling in thoughts. It's comforting, like having a twenty-four-hour positive support team that dispenses kind thoughts and unconditional love.

Often I'm sent to be the interpreter for people God can't reach through normal channels. They may be getting their own messages but don't know who's calling or know how to access call-waiting.

This job is listed on my spiritual resume as "The Last Stop on the Train." The number is 1-800-ULISTEN.

Spiritual Resume
Jane Ellis Conrad

In my lifetime God has given me a multitude of assignments with a variety of titles. Here is my spiritual resume.

Master Earth Angel (9/96 to present)
Prerequisite: Earth Angel Apprenticeship
Dispenses divine messages and touch globally through hands, books, songs, art, speeches, Internet. Assigned to the masses and some individuals.
Compensation: Unlimited fulfillment, gratification, and love
Employer: God
Call: 1-800-SERVICE

Earth Angel (4/4/55 to 9/96)
Hears and relays peaceful, loving, joyful spiritual messages. Available twenty-four hours a day, seven days a week to go wherever, whenever, with whomever, for whatever on a moment's notice. Open mind to receive Voice-activated messages, songs, poems, art. Appears unexpected, leaves undetected. Dispenses kind words, encouragement, unconditional love. Often assigned to individuals in need.
Education: Ongoing. Student of life.
Compensation: Unlimited happiness, joy, and love
Employer: God
Call: 1-800-DEARGOD

Spiritual Yellow Pages (1/90 to present)
A hub around which people revolve. Spiritual matchmaker. Soul connector. Clearinghouse. Performs Random Acts of Kindness. Dispenses Stones of Endless Possibilities.

Compensation: Unlimited friendship, harmony, and love
Employer: God
Call: 1-800-MATCHUP

Last Stop on the Train (1/90 to present)
Sent to people God can't reach through normal channels.
Interpreter. Friend. Mentor.
Compensation: Unlimited exhilaration, understanding, and love
Employer: God
Call: 1-800-ULISTEN

Cosmic Garbage Collector (1/90 to present)
Relieves earthlings of garbage collected over their lifetimes.
Burning bowl. Dream book. Smudge. Emotional and spiritual tuneup. Magnetic massage.
Compensation: Unlimited relief, forgiveness, and peace
Employer: God
Call: 1-800-CRAPGON

When my work on earth is done, this will be my final assignment.
Greeter at the Gate
Heavenly job. Works with Saint Peter to greet souls arriving in heaven from earth. Unlimited energy and enthusiasm. Lives in love. Appears as Angel in clouds. Whispers in ears. Blows wind through hair. Dispenses body "tinglies."
Education: Master of communication and life science
Compensation: Unlimited ecstasy and bliss
Employer: God
No call needed; I already have the job.

I asked God how long I would be on earth. God responded, "until your memory is stronger than your presence, then you will come home to the ultimate reunion."

The Gift of Joy

It's been said God works in mysterious ways. He sends us love in a variety of packages when we need it most.

Late one night while driving home from a meeting, my inner voice told me to take an alternate route. As I turned onto the five-lane highway for my final approach to home, I spotted a small, black object in the left-turn lane. Not knowing what it was, I drove around it and turned into my subdivision. Then the message came, "Go back and see what that is."

I drove back, pulled alongside, and opened my door. Staring up at me through one eye and a bloody face was a long-haired, black-and-white kitten. Without hesitation, I scooped up the ball of fur and put it in the basket I use for mail. I stopped at a convenience store across the street for cat food, kitty litter, and milk. I didn't have cats because I was allergic to them, but those seemed like essential items to buy.

The poor little thing lay so still I knew it was in shock. I already knew the reaction my West Highland terrier, Becky, would have when I brought this intruder into her domain. I was right—her curiosity and blood pressure quickly rose to elevated levels as her hunting instincts surfaced and she looked at the kitty as her next meal.

I gently washed the blood off the kitten's face. When it breathed, blood come out its nose. I figured it might have internal injuries. Only one eye was open, and it was focused on me. Every once in a while the kitten would open its mouth and a faint hiss would come out. I put a little dish of milk in the basket. No interest. I put some water on my finger and touched its mouth. Still no interest.

I started to pray. "Dear God, there must be a reason why you sent this precious kitty to me. If you let it live, I promise I'll take care of it." I put the basket and kitty in the bathtub and closed the bathroom door so Becky wouldn't bother it. Then I went to bed.

The next morning, just as I was waking up, I heard a faint mewing. I bounded out of bed and headed toward the sound with Becky right on my heels.

The kitten was alive. "Thank you, God. Please guide my hands and let me know what to do next."

Throughout the day I checked the kitten. It didn't move much and still hadn't taken any milk or water, so at 3:30 P.M. I headed for the vet with the kitty and Becky in tow. Everyone made quite a fuss over the three of us. Apparently they like people who rescue animals and keep them.

The technician washed the rest of the blood off the kitty's face and put a warm compress over the area where the second eye should have been. A moment later, the eye popped open. They did a thorough checkup and found no broken bones or internal injuries. Apparently it had been at least two days since the kitten had anything to eat or drink, so they put it on an IV and pumped kitten food into its mouth with a syringe.

"What's her name?" the technician asked. I sought divine inspiration. The Voices came: "Joyful!" "Her name is Joy," I replied.

My precious package of joy has long black fur, four white feet, a white chest and a partly white face, long curly ear hair, long whiskers, two green eyes, and a black heart on the end of her pink nose. Becky and Joy are best pals. They chase each other around and wrestle and can often be found in the dog bed or on my bed sleeping snuggled up together.

When I do paperwork in bed, Becky curls up on my lap and Joy lies on my chest and purrs loudly. Or sometimes she'll sit on my chest, stare into my eyes, and ever so gently pat my face with her paw. For whatever reason, I'm not allergic to this cat.

The first couple of weeks I had Joy, four friends offered to take her. One friend who doesn't even like cats wanted her. I told each person that I appreciated their kind offer but God had sent Joy to me. Although I enjoy giving things away, Joy was given to me to share with others but to keep for myself—to love, care for, and enjoy.

Each day I thank God for adding Joy to my life.

Angels Among Us

Although I know lots of other Earth Angels walking among us, one child stands out in my mind. Her name is Ann. I met her father several years before I had the pleasure of meeting her at a Saturday business seminar.

She was seven years old and had red, curly, shoulder-length hair, bright twinkling green eyes, and a warm smile that melts hearts. She is a wise old soul residing in the body of a child.

I asked her what she saw when she looked at me. Her eyes lit up and she said, "I see bright white light all around you." I asked her to draw what she saw. In just a few minutes, she drew an angel with an aura, feathered wings, halo, and big healing hands. She also hears singing in her head. When she started singing, it was the same music that comes through me. Beautiful songs in high angelic voices.

She told me a story about being with her friend in church and seeing her deceased grandfather appear surrounded by angels. "Tell your mama that I died instantly and didn't suffer," he said. He was a farmer and was killed by a machine called a "corn picker." Ann's mother was relieved to hear this message. Ann's parents had the wisdom and common sense to listen to her story and not be afraid of what they were hearing. Her friend was not so fortunate. Her parents were upset with her revelation and told her not to talk about it again. She lost the spiritual connection.

When I was ten years old, I told a minister that my mind was blank except when I heard messages. He told me it was impossible to have nothing going on in my head. Unfortunately, I thought he must be right and never mentioned it again, until I became an adult and knew better. My mind functions in a state of peace. If Spirit is not talking, I am not hearing anything unless I intentionally call in a thought. It's peaceful for me, yet I don't think most people would understand the feeling, living as we do in a world of turmoil.

How many God-given gifts are left unwrapped because the mind is closed to endless possibilities?

Time to Go

I fell asleep in the chair last night while writing. It was only 8:30 P.M., but my body was exhausted. Not from a hard day of physical work, but maybe from the end of a very brief, intense relationship that we both asked God for. Once each of us learned our lessons, we both needed to move on. Especially me.

God gave me the gift of touch. He works through me to relieve discomfort from the body and soul. People come to me. I help them be well. The only thing I ask them to do is help someone else however that's right for them. They start out strangers, then quickly become friends.

My heart is so sad because my friends and family hardly ever ask me to help them. Some of them have back problems, sleep problems, injuries, diseases, and other discomforts. I've offered to help. They would rather relinquish their power and responsibility to doctors than take charge of their own bodies and lives. Why don't they realize that good health is an inside job?

When I share my frustration with friends, the response has always been the same: "You can't be a prophet in your own land." I really didn't fully understand until yesterday when my friend said, "Jesus performed no miracles in Jerusalem."

I trust that God will move me to where I can best serve.

Healing Touch

I had just finished meditating and was pulling the covers up around my neck when my ten fingers started rapidly pulsating.

The Voices came: "If you question the power you've been given, then lay your left hand over the bump on your right arm and see what happens."

The bump was round, about a half-inch in diameter and one-eighth inch high. It had been on my forearm for more than ten years. Since skin cancer runs in my family, I look at it every day. Sometimes it's white and scaly, other times dark brown. Or bloody when I pick it. I laid my hand just over, but not touching, the bump. My middle finger started pulsating, so I laid it on the bump for less than a minute. Then I fell asleep.

In the morning I woke up and looked at the bump. Half of it was gone completely, and the remaining part had shrunk to half its height. Within three days, the bump had vanished. There was no scar or skin discoloration to indicate that the bump had ever been there!

Am I wearing God's hands?

God's Conduit

As I drove away from the funeral home, with my face flushed and hands burning, I thanked God for letting me be a conduit for His energy and love. So many times I arrive just as some trauma is taking place, or the person unknowingly waits until I'm there before their distress starts.

The woman at the funeral home was there to pay last respects to her sister-in-law, who was my friend Bob's mother. Bob's wife, Kathy, is also clairvoyant and I asked her if she knew her mother-in-law was leaving. "Yes, I got the message a couple of months ago but didn't tell Bob. Bob felt her leaving about a week ago. She had been in a nursing home for eleven years, was blind, and had Alzheimer's disease for the past five." Kathy and I talked about all the people who had left in the past few months—my mother two months prior; my sister-in-law's father the previous week; Bob's mother the day before; and a rash of other people. Deaths seem to happen in clumps—usually three at a time.

I started talking about this aunt as if I knew her. "She is kind and compassionate, everyone's best friend, the matriarch of the family, an angel." Kathy agreed with everything Spirit was saying through me. I noticed the glow around her. Kathy and I talked about five more minutes about other things as I prepared to go home. But the commotion around this woman drew my attention. She was in distress. I stood about twenty feet away, with my palms facing her, and sent white light.

It was two or three minutes before Spirit sent me the message to offer my assistance. It came not in words but in motion. I was being physically moved toward her. Her face was chalk white, the blood had drained away. Her energy was gone and she was in trouble. I stood in front of her and asked, "Would you like me to help? I do Reiki." No one understood what I was offering. "I do energy work. I have healing hands. Would you like me to help?"

The woman grabbed my hands and pleaded, "Pray for me!"

I closed my eyes and prayed, "Mother, Father, God, send the white light of your energy and love through me to help this beautiful soul to be well. Keep her safe in your loving care and grant her peace." As I prayed, the heat came pulsing through my hands and face, warming my body like a sauna. Sometimes I have so much heat, perspiration drips off my face and makes my clothes wet. I whispered, "Take my energy."

She made a sound somewhere between a sigh and a gasp. I know she felt what I did, as the energy transferred from my body to hers. I put my two hands over the top of her head for a minute then moved behind her to Reiki her shoulders and heart. I wanted to put a hand on her heart from the front but didn't because she might have been embarrassed having a hand on her chest in public so I got to her heart from her back. "Thank you," she said. This was echoed by her concerned children.

"God be with you," I said, as I moved toward Bob and Kathy's last hugs and goodbyes. I knew what had just happened was better than any other words of condolence or cards of sympathy that I could have given Bob. He was my husband's friend from high school and didn't abandon me after our marriage ended, unlike some of the other couples with whom my husband and I socialized.

As I drove away from the funeral home with total gratitude, joy, and love, I talked to God. "I am so honored and grateful to be in your service. I surrender to your will. How can I serve you better? I'm available. This is the best job in the whole world. But it's not even a job—it's a pleasure. I'm so happy." Even though my face and hands felt like they had been sunburned, I was grateful for my life's work.

I thought about two other instances where I had been sent to help. One was between church services. The second service had just started. I walked toward the coatrack when a friend rushed up and said, "Go into the bathroom. Someone needs your help!" Off I went.

A woman in her forties, wearing a royal blue dress, was sitting in a chair with a another woman's face about five inches away firing questions at her: "How long have you had the chest pains and shortness of breath? Are you here with someone? Do you have a history of heart problems?" Her voice faded as the woman in the blue dress grabbed my right hand and held tight, like I was her lifeline. My left hand started to Reiki her heart. I know she felt God's energy coming through me. Her panic turned to peace as we waited for EMS to arrive.

A doctor from the congregation helped the five paramedics and firefighters ask questions, start an IV, and prepare her for transport to the hospital. I gave her a Stone of Endless Possibilities, and she clung to it. The stretcher came in, and I went outside the door and waited. As they wheeled her out, her eyes were darting all over until she spotted me. "You're going to be fine," I reassured her. She knew that.

Another time I was with my friend Elaine and was told to take a walk in the park. As I parked the car and started to walk, the sound of sirens was getting closer and closer. The EMS truck pulled into the park as I noticed a blonde woman in her twenties lying facedown on a blanket with a few people helplessly scurrying around. I stopped, raised my palms toward her, and started sending light. Elaine, who is a nurse, asked me what Spirit said was wrong with her.

"Spirit said it was a reaction between something she drank and prescription drugs she had taken," I said.

This young woman was unconscious and in trouble. The paramedics started an IV, checked her vital signs, and within five minutes she was in the vehicle being taken away, while her boyfriend and other relatives who had arrived consoled each other, then left. Spirit had moved me down the path about fifty yards away, but with clear access, to send light and energy. Elaine loves being with me because she enjoys these adventures as much as I do. It's being on call twenty-four hours a day, seven days a week, and not knowing where I'll be, what I'll be doing, or with whom. It's just being ready, willing, and able to serve.

Songs From the Angels

The songs keep coming…and coming…and coming. Very high angelic voices. Beautiful songs. The words come out intact. No editing needed. Thank you, God, for angel songs. They are a source of pleasure and fill my heart with joy.

Random Acts of Kindness (Hearts Entwined Throughout the World) came through me while attending Alan Cohen's Mastery Training in Maui, Hawaii, in August 1995. Fortunately, I was close to a piano and captured the melody. Here you may enjoy the lyrics.

Random Acts of Kindness (Hearts Entwined Throughout the World)

Hearts entwined throughout the world,
Bringing peace and joy,
Spreading Love and harmony,
And goodwill to man.

Hearts entwined throughout the world,
Kindness now abounds,
Smiles and laughter fill the air,
Sisterhood of man.

(CHORUS)
Random Acts of Kindness be,
Catalysts for Peace,
We're joined in friendship, bound in Love,
And in harmony.

Hearts entwined throughout the world,
Random acts are done,
Kindness spreads to all the world,
Peace is now at hand.

Caring, Sharing, Laughter, Love,
Friendship, Peace and Joy,
We pass from darkness into light,
Finally—Peace On Earth.

(CHORUS)

(CHORUS)

Words and music through Jane Ellis Conrad, with additional music by Judith Pearce Powell. Produced and performed by Judith Peace Powell, 1996. To obtain a copy of Kristen Hartnagel's version on her tape *Who Do You Want to Be?*, see page 109.

Chevette Shove

I get several calls a week from people who want advice, healing touch, or just an ear to listen. They may be strangers who were telling someone their problems and were told to call me. Counseling is not my profession, but I dispense spiritual messages and advice when asked. It's like the words come out of my mouth without going through my brain. I'm just the conduit. God is the source.

Since I am a Spiritual Yellow Pages, I often refer them to others that may give them more help. Often, they have slipped off their path, and just need a Chevette shove.

THE JOYFUL JOURNEY OF AN EARTH ANGEL

In the 1970s, I had a yellow Chevrolet Chevette Sand-piper. It was a small compact car that was like driving a roller skate with a steering wheel. It sounded like a giant bee buzz-ing! Zzzzzzzz. But it was a great car for maneuvering through traffic and parking in any available crack. One cold winter day I was driving down an icy side street when all of a sudden I stopped. The car was so light that the wheels were spinning but I wasn't moving. A man walking on the sidewalk stepped into the street and gave my Chevette a shove. My journey continued. Zzzzzzzzz.

Sometimes all it takes is a few words, a gentle touch with words or an embrace to get someone back on track. Zzzzzzzzz.

Signs and Messages

My life has been wonderful.
Partly because of the cards I was dealt.
But mostly because I listened,
To how they were to be played.

Jane Ellis Conrad, August 1994

Forgiveness, Love,
Mind Your Own Business

Faced with a challenge? Where do you go for help? I just close my eyes, open my heart, and head to God.

Did you know that God and the angels are unemployed unless asked for help? They will not interfere with your free will. If a question is never asked, the answer is always no.

Just surrender to God and see what happens. The answer may not be the one you expect. Earth can be a good or bad place depending on your thoughts and attitude. Heaven is ONLY Good! There is no unemployment. One big happy family, just like it should be on earth. Heaven is what life is all about…caring, sharing, laughter, and love. Plus there are plenty of vacancies.

When you leave earth to "go home," you could be an angel in the clouds, the wind through someone's hair, the warm feeling of love, or the one who's whispering words of encouragement and hope. I've asked God to let me be the

"greeter" at the gate with Saint Peter. That's my ideal assignment. I'd smile and hug each new arrival. "Hi. Nice to see
you again. You really made a difference on earth. Now the
journey continues."

Life can be so easy, yet people make it so hard. To have
joy, harmony, and peace of mind, all you have to do is remember six words: forgiveness, love, mind your own business.

Relayed Message

"You have to help me find my mom. My grandma just
died." It was Kristen on the phone, the daughter of my friend,
Barb.

I told her, "I don't know where she's staying, just that
she's in Lillydale, New York, attending Alan Cohen's seminar. I'll make some calls and call you back."

"Okay, angels," I said. "Where do I start?" The Voice came,
"Call Maui and find out where Alan is staying." Fortunately,
Alan's office was still open, and I received the name of the
New York contact. Again I was lucky to have someone an-
swer the phone. "I have to reach someone who is attending
Alan Cohen's seminar. There's been a death in the family."

"Good luck. There are two hotels and lots of bed and
breakfasts in and out of town. Chances are you won't find
her." Those were not encouraging words, but then she didn't
know whom she was talking to or the connections I have.
She gave me phone numbers for the two hotels.

I called the first hotel. "Do you have anyone registered
from Michigan?" They didn't. I dialed the second number.
"Do you have anyone registered from Michigan?" Barb was
there.

I relayed the message to her to call home but didn't tell her why. That wasn't my job. I only needed to find her and pass on the message.

Barb wasn't actually staying at that hotel. She was there to meet with someone. On her way through the lobby she heard the desk clerk say Michigan and went over to ask who they were looking for. She called home and got the message that her mother had died.

Coincidence or fate? Just *is*.

This job is listed on my Spiritual Resume as: "Spiritual Yellow Pages." I'm a hub around which people revolve. A spiritual matchmaker and soul connector. The number is 1-800-MATCHUP.

Dollars From Heaven

God gives me assignments and often supplies the money to accomplish the tasks.

I was sent to a bookstore where a wide variety of angel books were on display. Karen Goldman's *Angel Book* caught my eyes. It was filled with a lot of good spiritual information but I thought the eighteen-dollar price tag was more than I could afford. The message came: "Buy the book, the money will follow." With sheer faith the money was pulled from my wallet in exchange for this wonderful book.

The next day I went to an auto plant to pick up some spare parts. (I had a job as coordinator of spare parts for an auto supplier.) As I backed the van into the loading dock, the message came: "Go look behind the guard railing that's protecting the wall from the trucks." I looked behind the railing and spotted two one-hundred-dollar bills folded and laying on the ground. I picked up the money and went back to the van. As I hyperventilated with excitement, I asked God if the money should be turned in. "No," came the reply. "Whoever lost it doesn't know they lost it. Go back; there's more."

I almost ran back to the railing. This time there was a fifty-dollar bill lying on the ground. It was folded just like the other bills. I returned to the van and with deep gratitude said, "Thank you, God, for the money. What do you want me to do with it? Do you want me to gamble with it?"

"No," came the reply.

"Do you want me to save it?"

"No. You never save talents. You must first give in order to receive."

"What do you want me to do with it?" I asked.

"Start another company off your existing company and call it Daisy Jane. This company will publish spiritual messages that will be sent through you in the future." That was the seed money to start my company that published some of my art and music.

Another time I was getting out of my car on the way to a business meeting. The ground beside my car was covered with fifty-five bright, shiny pennies. Other times I find dollars, quarters, dimes, nickels, and pennies and throw them into a glass container of "found money." When the pot exceeds twenty dollars, I buy someone a gift or perform a Random Act of Kindness, such as anonymously paying for a senior citizen's meal at a restaurant. The expression on the recipient's face is priceless. Whenever I give with no expectations of getting anything back, miracles happen. I found it true that givers get.

Life Is...

While driving to a meeting, I asked my guides for a definition of recognition. "We'll do better than that, we'll give you a definition of life. Rip open a bank envelope and draw the following in six panels.

Life is...
Blue sky, brown dirt, and a seed—call it *inspiration*
Rain coming down on the seed—call it *action*
A red flower growing—call it *achievement*
The sun shining on the flower—call it *recognition*
A full-blown flower garden—call it *success*
Two flowers dying, sending seeds
into the ground—call it *regeneration*
...life goes on."

I asked what I was to do with this information and was told to "make a paper collage calendar in bright colors. Sign and number each copy and supply a certificate of authenticity. Print five thousand."

But I wasn't given a marketing plan. I tried to sell them for ten dollars without success. So I asked for guidance. The Voices came: "If you can't sell them for what they're worth, give them away."

Once I released the need to sell them and started handing them out, the orders came. I gave away more than six hundred during Random Acts of Kindness week, which is celebrated every year during the second week in February. I also gave them to hospital patients and staff on Christmas Day when I caroled in my angel dress. I gave them to anyone else in need of inspiration.

My God Is...

What does your God look like? Want to hear about mine?

- My God is a peaceful loving feeling I call Mother, Father, God, Light.
- My God is ever present, all day every day, rain, snow, sleet, hail, sunshine, blue skies, rainbows.
- My God resides in my heart—we are one.
- My God said everyone can make a direct connection and doesn't need to go through anyone else.
- My God told me not to care about how anyone else finds Him/Her and they are not to care what I believe either.
- My God said it's okay if I want to go to church and worship with others or sit beside a cool, swift stream, or look into the eyes of a child or animal or beautiful, fragrant flower.
- My God is everywhere in everything.
- My God loves the songs the angels sing to me and the joy-filled smile on my face when I'm singing, dancing, writing, or just meditating, loving life, and appreciating each breath.
- My God is happy that I answered the call to serve in a most creative way.
- My God is glad I love all my businesses, and sends love and light to all my customers and distributors.
- My God loves me to pass out Stones of Endless Possibilities and tell people whatever they dream, believe, and put action to they can achieve because they are limitless.
- My God loves me unconditionally.

- My God wants me to be wealthy so I can live well, be an example for others, and help people and charities in need.

- My God doesn't tell me what to do, how to do, when to do, just sits back and offers encouragement, support, and unconditional love.

- My God wants me to be the best I can be and help others be their best.

- My God told me there are no mistakes or sins, just lessons to learn on my journey through life.

- My God wants me to sing like an angel, dance like there is life-force energy in my feet, and write from my heart.

- My God wants me to do Random Acts of Kindness without anyone knowing.

- My God gently wakes me up each morning with words of encouragement, joy, and solitude.

- My God has been telling me for years to be quiet and listen to the silence, and keeps sending the message knowing one day I will learn that lesson.

- My God loves to hear me laugh and tell people I'm thinking about them and sending my love and appreciation for their friendship.

- My God is patient when my ego starts to emerge and have an opinion about what someone else is doing, and I comment, "Sorry, God, I wasn't judging, just making an observation."

- My God loves to hear me wake up each morning and say, "Good Morning, Mother, Father, God. Thank you for another day of life. I surrender to your will. Not my will but thine be done. How can I serve you today and every day. Send the people to me who you want me to help—and me to them. I release all need to control the outcome. Thank you, God, for another perfect day. I love you."

- My God gave me six words that, at all times, when remembered and practiced, will give me peace of mind. *Forgiveness, love, mind my own business.*

- My God sends me challenges to learn, grow, and maximize my potential.

- My God wants me to touch people through positive actions and words, and offers to empty the garbage bags they were given at birth.

- My God wants to me be a Spiritual Yellow Pages where people can come and get connected with whomever and whatever they need for inspiration and growth.

- My God has called me "the last stop on the train." When people are getting messages and not paying attention, or not knowing what they are hearing, I will be an interpreter.

- My God told me that eternity is now. The breath in my lungs right now is all I'm guaranteed.

- My God uses my heart, soul, hands, and voice to help people be well physically, emotionally, and spiritually.

Oh, how easy and peaceful it is to be one with *my God*.

"Tinglies"

God is very patient. I was rocking in my big, padded, pink writing chair with my feet on a filing box facing heaven out the window talking to God. "I'm ready to go, be, see, and do whatever you have planned for my life. You and my team of archangels, angels, teachers, guides, and my Guardian Angel, Gabriella Faith, have carte blanche. You don't need me to ask for help. Just tell me whenever you want me to change course."

Spirit interrupted my words with "I smell the smells (candles), hear the sounds (bubbling waterfall, the Pachelbel Canon), and feel your love all around (peaceful).

"Hold on one minute," I said." Let me start a new page on my computer. Okay, I'm ready."

Silence.

"Is that it?"I asked.

"That's it," they said. "Just write what you sense—see, hear, taste, touch, feel. Here's one more line. See the beauty in your midst (flowers)."

Do you ever get "tinglies" when you hear something? That is God's validation that what you're hearing is right and true. It may be slight, like the breeze that makes the hair on your arms stand up. Or a power surge of blood that starts at your feet and blasts through your body and makes your head feel like it's going to explode. I've even had some surges that run up and down and up and down, head to toe. That's when there is no doubt that God is sending a mega message, special delivery, no thinking necessary. Ears only...just listen to the silence and breathe. The answers will come before the questions are asked.

———•◆•◆•◆•———

Hallmark

This morning started off like all the rest with Spirit planning the day and reviewing lessons learned from the previous day. "Send your Save the Children packet to the president of Hallmark Cards. Also ask Hallmark to make the Christmas card you have been using for the past three years into a permanent note card. It is a beautiful card with an angel embracing the world with the message inside: 'Love the world to peace.'" I used the card year around until I ran out.

I remembered another Hallmark message I received in 1995 when I was awakened from a sound sleep with a poem being dictated. Normally I would have had a pad of paper next to the bed but it wasn't there. "Hold on" I pleaded. "I need to find some paper." I opened up my desk drawer, found only stationery and greeting cards, and thought, "I can't use this; it's stationery." The Voice came, "It's paper! Use it, and next time buy Hallmark, and send the very best." Angel humor.

The World Mourns...
Heaven Rejoices

I asked God, "Why Diana? Why now?"

She had finally found the love that had eluded her for thirty-six years. The Voices came: "Once her memory was stronger than her presence she was free to leave, to escape the paparazzi who made her life on earth a living hell. She was propelled from an operating table into the peaceful energy of a loving God. No more flashbulbs, rudeness, or danger. Just love, peace, contentment, and joy. Nothing will ever hurt her again."

Just close your eyes and visualize what Diana might have seen and felt the night her lights went out. Flashing bulbs. Paparazzi. Dinner. Friendship ring. Love. Relentless paparazzi. Flashing bulbs. Speeding car. Loud crash. Sudden stop. Breaking glass. Tearing metal. Crushing bones. Flashing bulbs. Surgeons. Darkness. *Bright light*. No flashing bulbs. Golden path. Peace at last. Daddy's smile. Dodi's kiss. Ultimate escape. No flashing bulbs. No high-speed chase. Peace and joy.

No paparazzi. No flashing bulbs. Love story continued. Another place and time. No flashing bulbs. Free at last.

The world was shocked and mourned her death. But why was I calm? Why wasn't I crying like everyone else? Instead of sadness I felt only an inner peace. I felt what she felt. Not sorrow like the rest of the world, but rather exhilaration and freedom. Diana, Princess of Wales, was free at last!

She gave more than she took, helped rather than hindered. And in the end, when it looked as if she had finally found love, God called her home.

Flowers were piled high around the palace she called home. Notes were scribbled, and tears shed. The world stopped for an instant to remember this angel of peace who had touched more lives than even she could imagine. God called her home to a safe haven. She had served her causes and mankind well. Now her journey in human form had ended.

Diana need not worry about her beloved sons, William and Harry. They share her blood and her heart. Her causes will become theirs. Her sons may not understand why she had to die, but they will remember her love and how she lived. Good people of the world will protect them from the factions that dogged her to death.

Be at peace, Diana, Princess of Wales. You touched our hearts.

A week after Princess Diana departed, Mother Teresa made the trip. Again, I was filled with inner peace rather than tears. "Why now, God?"

The Voices came, "Princess Diana became the diversion Mother Teresa had been waiting for. Her healing work was done in God's name. She wanted no fanfare or sadness at her death. Diana's funeral drew attention to the front door so Mother Teresa could slip out the back."

In one short week the world lost two Angels of Peace. Heaven is celebrating jobs well-done by these extraordinary women from two different worlds. Their hearts were joined together in one common purpose. They helped where needed and left this world better than they had found it. God called—they answered.

Through their deaths we learned about life. Does this story sound familiar?

Revelation

This morning while I was meditating in bed, I tried to remember when my Voices started coming. The year 1955 flashed before my eyes. That's when I had the revelation.

April 4, 1955 (4-4-55) was the day my paternal grandfather, Robert Henry Ellis, died. I remember him as a frail, cheerful man with thin gray hair and suspenders to hold his pants up. He had leukemia for five years. Both arms were black-and-blue from all the shots and transfusions he endured, but an unshakable belief in God was with him to the end as he sang *Beautiful Savior* with my dad at his side. I wondered if he finished the song before being swept into the tunnel of white light…peace…no more pain. The Voices started when my grandfather passed.

Since I'm in tune with my spiritual helpers, I've often asked these beings to identify themselves so our encounters would be "up close and personal." For years I've had a guide named Harry. He was a teacher and great comfort to me whenever I needed advice. I must have been sleeping over the years to not realize that Harry was my Grandpa Ellis. Although his proper name was Robert, everyone called him Harry.

"I'm sorry, Grandpa, for not realizing it was you. You were the one who got me through the cancer and the turmoil in my marriage. And the one who whispered in my ear, 'God

loves you, Janie. You are the messenger and have no limits.
Be an example for others to follow. Go in peace.' All along, I
thought Dad and Grandma Ellis were guiding me…and it was
you, Grandpa."

I felt as if another door opened that day and I had risen to
another level of spiritual awareness—energized and invincible,
and more determined than ever to listen to my Voices and
act on what I'm told to do.

For a moment I thought about my last day on earth.
Whenever anyone tells me to have a good day, I reply, "If I'm
breathing, it's a good day." Then one day another thought
was added to this response: "It will be a fantastic day when
I'm not breathing, because I'm *going home* (to God)."

Visits From Dad

Ah, bliss at last. It had been a very long day. The Voices
came: "Get out of bed and journal what has happened lately.
There were some significant events and you can't let them go
unrecorded."

I put aside the book I was reading, turned on the computer, and began writing about what had happened when I'd
been standing in my dining room looking outside. The doorbell rang, my dog Becky barked and ran to the door. I was
staring at the porch. The doorbell was pushed in as if someone were ringing it but there was no *physical* body on the
porch.

For an instant I thought about the bell at the back door.
Then I realized that I had no back door, just the double front
doors I was looking at. I opened the door to fix the bell, but it
was no longer depressed.

A strong wind rushed by me into the living room. My body tingled. *This must surely be a God moment!* Then the date flashed before my eyes. May 5, 1996. Peacefulness came over me. My dad had died one year ago today. "Hi, Dad," I sighed. "So nice to get a physical sign from you. You're always in my heart and thoughts."

Suddenly I was transported back in time. A few months earlier, I had been in a Catholic church for the funeral of a friend's mother. As I studied the huge crucifix, it seemed odd that there were no spikes in Jesus's hands or feet. Then I looked away for a little while; and when I looked back, I saw spikes in *both* hands *and* feet. They weren't little spikes that I could have missed. These spike heads were at least two inches in diameter. I asked my Higher Being what it meant, then sat very still with my hands open, resting on each knee.

The Voices came: "The absence of spikes symbolizes the perfect Christ that lies within you, my child. Your heart is pure and your intent sincere. God is in your heart and your soul. You will be protected and cared for. For you are the Messenger of Peace."

Suddenly I realized Dad was visiting me to bring peace to my soul and rest to my body. Dad was my hero. He had raised me to believe I could do anything I wanted to do. If I could dream it, I could achieve it. He was a registered architect in thirty-seven states with only a high school diploma—quite a self-made success! He taught me not to sell products but rather to build relationships. He treated everyone as if he had known them forever. It didn't matter if the person was a president, engineer, mechanic, or cab driver—as long as they were decent human beings, they were all his friends. He grew up in an era when milk and baked goods were delivered house-to-house. So he jokingly told his customers, "I just want to be your milkman. Great products, reliable service, friendly personnel, and prices you can afford."

We were all blessed by my dad's presence and touched by his soul. He sold himself as a package, not flashy or ostentatious, but gentle and kind, caring and supportive. But most of all funny. Very, very funny. God did us all a big favor by sending my dad. He cared...he shared...he laughed...and he loved with all his heart. He was the original Mr. Random Acts of Kindness. He was doing Random Acts of Kindness long before books were written about them and yearly events were set up to promote the concept. He was always buying dinners, groceries, and presents for family, friends, and strangers. What a guy!

I started to think about the celebration of life we had at church after my dad died. He didn't want anyone to wear black, cry, or be sad at his passing. In spite of serious health challenges in the previous several years, he maintained a positive attitude and continued to tell jokes to anyone who crossed his path. The celebration was just as my mind had planned it over the previous two years. That was when he had the first of several strokes. I wrote his eulogy and started preparing myself for the day the news would come that he was gone. Friends, family, and colleagues saw him in different settings but all remember him in the same way. He treated everyone like a good friend. That's why it had to be a joyful event to celebrate his life not mourn his death.

Before the service, I sat quietly and asked Dad if there were any messages he wanted me to deliver along with my own written words. His voice came, "Tell them I was stubborn and used *can't* as a motivator, not a deterrent. Tell them I raised you as a person instead of a female and set no limitations. You could be anything you wanted to be, do anything you wanted to do. The sky was the limit. Before you begin your love message, tell them your Dad is *still* giving, and hold up a red ribbon that says *Who I am makes a difference*. Give a ribbon and a Little Miracle card to each outstretched hand.

Tell them that, if they ever think that one person can't make a difference, they should remember this day."

In some ways my dad was progressive, in others so old-fashioned. Although he always said I could do anything, I believe that in his mind he thought I would get married, have children, and stay home to raise them as my Mom had done with me. He never talked to me about being an architect or engineer or taking over his share of the company when he retired. My brother was the caretaker of that dream. All those eggs were in my brother's basket.

Unfortunately, my brother didn't get registered as an architect or engineer before my dad had to retire, so control of the company was forfeited to non-family members. I know that Dad was saddened to see his dream slip through his fingers. More than once I've looked up to heaven and asked, "Why not me, Dad? You said I could be anything I wanted. Why didn't you let me be the caretaker of your dream?" I guess I never expressed an interest in becoming an architect or engineer even though I loved math. Too late now, but I'm going to make a difference, Dad. I'm going to help people be well. I'm going to do Random Acts of Kindness. Just like you!

Release to Peace

Helpless. Heartbreaking. Just a few of the emotions I felt watching my mother agonize over the death of my father. She was lost. Confused. Terrified. Angry. She would lie in bed and rock from side to side with covers over her head crying "Oh, God. Oh, God. Oh, God" And under my breath I would join her and add my own words, "Oh, God. Let her go. Take her soon. I love her. Please don't make her suffer in a body and mind that serve her no purpose. She was a wonderful, productive, caring, compassionate woman. Please don't make her suffer."

Unfortunately, she did suffer. Alzheimer's had already set in before my dad passed. I believe that was the reason he lasted longer than he could have. There were so many chances for him to leave. Several strokes that left him disabled, unable to get his thoughts out, walk with the swiftness as before, be the life of the party, or the comedian on the golf course. He could remember only a few jokes now, and those he repeated over and over. Mom laughed like it was the first time she'd heard them...and maybe it was.

Her mother went the same way. After my grandfather died of lung cancer, from years of abusing his body with cigarette addiction, my grandmother went into fear and denial and got Alzheimer's disease. Webster should use this definition for cigarettes: "When used as intended, can cause you and those around you great physical and emotional harm and possibly kill you."

I remember my mother's frustration with my grandmother. Grandma lived five out of her last ten years in a nursing home. The final two years she was tied to her chair or in bed so she wouldn't wander around, fall down, and hurt herself.

On Thanksgiving Day, I went with my Dad to pick up Grandma for dinner. He said she didn't know we were coming yet she answered the door with her rain coat on. She was never invited ahead of time because she would have said "No." So we just showed up. She always wore the raincoat over multiple layers of clothes.

One day I went with Mom and Dad to take Grandma out for a ride. When Grandma took her coat off, I couldn't hold back my laughter, so Dad took me outside. I didn't mean to hurt her feelings, but what I saw was too funny. Grandma had two blouses and two sweaters on top, and three pairs of pants on the bottom with her white underpants on the outside of the last pair of pants. She had all the pieces, and more than necessary, just in the wrong order according to the norm. Or did order matter? She was covered, which was better than later on, when she would take off all her clothes and streak. I think that's when they put her in the full-time nursing section.

Grandma swore like a truck driver, lashed out at anyone trying to help her, and hoarded milk taken from her meal tray in the cafeteria. She'd squirrel away the milk for a rainy day—in her underwear drawer, closet, purse, under the bed, on the heat register. The sour milk smell in her room would turn my stomach. I was more religious than spiritual back then and didn't know that she might have been saved years of turmoil had the family expressed their love and wished her a joyful journey to heaven.

My sister ended up taking my mom to California to live with her. They were joined at the hip from birth through death. I often felt like Mom only had one daughter, and it wasn't me. I was on the outside looking in as they shopped, laughed, and shuffled down the street arm in arm singing. Mom was the Girl Scout leader, church youth group sponsor, and total support system. And often frustrated parent, because my sister was also very demanding. It was easier to give her what she wanted rather than hear her yell and scream and call you names. That would be her albatross and keep me from having a close sister relationship with her until Mom died.

I went to California twice a year to visit and saw her slip from a confused mind with a healthy body, to a frail body with a mind that no longer could even speak. She, like her mother, would lash out at the loving nurses who would clean her up each day, comb her hair, and put her in a chair in the recreation room to visit with others in the same state. They were all probably thinking they were meeting each other for the first time. Maybe, maybe not.

By the time Mom entered the home, I had already received a message from God to be a hospice volunteer, to guide people to the light. What a wonderful organization. A whole team of medical people and volunteers that administer to the dying person and their family and give them comfort and peace on the last leg of their journey.

I've only been assigned two people besides my mom. Spirit said, "it was for your Mom that we wanted you to join." My first lady had cancer everywhere, and lasted two days. I only spoke to her twice, but was actually at her home to do healing touch on two of her daughters. The second lady had stomach cancer. I bought her food, massaged her back, and her daughter's back, too. I was sent for the families as much as the patients.

I didn't want anyone to know exactly when I was arriving at the nursing home, so I could be with Mom alone. After all, I had her attention for my first four years of life. Before her bones were brittle and touching her brought agony, I would comb her hair and rub her back. But most of all, I'd close my eyes, open my heart, and let God's words come through. "Mom, I love you. I appreciate all the values you instilled in me about honesty, compassion, responsibility, achievement, competition, teaching me to play golf, taking me on vacation, loving and supporting my dad's dreams to own his own company, providing a safe loving environment. I want you to be happy. So whenever you're ready, it's okay to release your soul from this body and be with God and Dad. Jim's okay. Marilyn's okay. I'm okay." Twice a year, for two years, I told her that in person. Several times a month, I'd tell her on the phone or in a letter. Her condition kept getting worse. After a while she couldn't walk. Then she couldn't talk. Then she wouldn't eat.

I kept asking my sister, "Did you tell mom it was okay to go?"

"Kinda," she'd say.

"There is no kinda, you have to say—Mom, I love you, it's okay to go to God and Dad."

It got so bad she had to wear morphine patches and couldn't stand to be touched or moved without wincing and crying out in pain. Spirit said, "Call your Mom, sing to her, and release her again." The nurse put the phone up to her, but there was no sound coming from her end, so I just kept talking. "Hi, Mom, this is Jane. How are you today? Just calling to tell you I love you." Then I started singing *Beautiful Savior,* hoping that would be the key to the vehicle to drive her home. That was the song my grandfather and father used to leave. Then I sang *The First Noel, O Come All Ye Faithful,* and other Christmas songs that came to mind. I didn't know that the nurse had me on the speaker phone and I was entertaining the entire area.

My sister was agonizing over Mom's pain, and again I asked, "Did you tell Mom it's okay to go? She's waiting for you. She already knows Jim and I are okay. You have to say the words."

About 6:30 A.M. on December 30, my Dad's voice woke me up and said he was coming to take Mom home. So I wasn't surprised when my sister called me about 1:30 P.M. to say "Mom's gone."

I asked, "Did you release her?"

She said, "Yes. I said I loved her and it's okay to go. I left to get something to eat. When I got back about a half hour later, the nurses were cleaning up her lifeless body. She was gone." Then the guilt set in as my sister cried, "Maybe she wouldn't have had to go through so much pain for so long if I had released her earlier. I didn't want her to think I didn't love her." I reassured her that it wasn't her fault. "Mom and

God decided the time and place her soul train would leave the station, not you."

How many souls have stayed longer than necessary because of fearing the unknown? All they have to do is surrender to God and relinquish their ticket. Fight the flight or release to peace?

———————————•✦•●•✦•———————————

Drumming

Thump, thump, thump. Thump, thump, thump. Sounds from the drum being beaten in a mesmerizing pattern. This was my first American Indian drumming ceremony—a real spiritual experience.

A dozen others shared the small, dimly lit back room at the metaphysical store in hopes of finding our spiritual animals. Flickering, sweet-smelling candles added to the inspiring atmosphere.

Twelve participants sprawled on the carpeted floor, eyes closed. Several dozen earth-toned pillows and blankets were used to soften the floor.

The master drummer showed us how to beat the drum to call up good spirits or drive bad ones away. All we had to do was become totally relaxed and melt into the floor—let our minds go blank, slip into twilight consciousness, and wait for our spiritual animal to appear. Our animal would be the one we made eye contact with.

Thump, thump, thump. As my body relaxed and sank deeper and deeper, the drum became softer and more distant. Within thirty seconds the animals started coming—raccoons, porcupines, wolves, cows, ducks, chickens, all walking single-file, like a zoo parade.

Then my beautiful guardian angel, Gabriella Faith, appeared. A white dove flew into her outstretched hands. The vision faded. An eagle appeared. I saw great strength as the big brown bird, with its huge wingspan and snowy white head, lifted off with determination and purpose. It soared upward, spreading its massive wings and pointing its uplifted head and beak toward heaven. I was on the ground viewing this magnificent creature when my body jolted. The eagle and I became one. I found myself looking down on earth and its inhabitants.

As I soared high above the earth, I could see the brutality and savagery in Bosnia, but the fighting stopped as I soared over the battlefields. People looked up to track my flight. I sent them blessings from above. They laid down their arms and joined hands in peace and harmony to watch the wind fill my wings and lift me to greater heights.

The drumming slowed down to a stop. Gradually we all got up and left the room for a ten-minute break. I was amazed at the journey I had just been on and was anxious to continue. As I stretched out on the floor with a pillow under my head and a rolled-up blanket under my bent knees, I quickly got in sync with the drum.

My journey continued. In came peacocks, llamas, bobcats, wolves, turtles, frogs, fish, skunks…then the eagle and I resumed our union. I flew past Mt. Rushmore and witnessed the beauty of Yellowstone. The pristine pastures in Idaho. Up into Canada, Lake Louise, and Banff. For an instant I flashed back and imagined what these two places had looked like forty years earlier, when my family had been heading to the region. Our camp stove had exploded in Mitchell, South Dakota, and my legs had been severely burned. Ten days in the hospital had ended our vacation and kept me from seeing the sights I now saw from the sky. One day I'll complete this journey on the ground.

Everywhere I flew, people stopped and looked to the heavens to see me fly. They forgot about wars and fighting and were filled with peace in their hearts and souls. Contentment and happiness were everywhere. I now know my purpose. Like this eagle, I am a messenger of peace.

I spotted a small Indian boy with big brown doe eyes and black hair. He looked up at me while his wise father explained the great messages brought by the eagle. My body jolted again and I was transformed from the eagle into the body of this little boy. I was actually watching the eagle through his eyes and was struck by its beauty. I had thought I was a pretty good-looking eagle, but from this viewpoint my magnificence was awesome!

In the distance I heard thumping. It grew louder and closer. The eagle flew off and faded from sight. A peaceful feeling enveloped my body. It would be exciting to share my experiences with the group, and I wondered what animals they saw.

Only three people out of twelve saw animals. The other two people saw one animal each. As my journey unfolded, I felt excited yet sad for the others. I'm sure I wasn't the only one to wonder why I saw all the animals and they didn't. I felt like apologizing for hoarding them all.

Then the Voices came, "Never apologize for your gifts and talents. When you work for anything, you deserve to own it, and not make excuses for others' lack. Results are based on our life's lessons and decisions. Your obedience to divine direction and inspiration has been rewarded in ways some people would not understand in their lifetime. If they want what you have, they need to earn it as you did. No freebies." This made me feel better.

The master drummer seemed impressed with my gifts. I had the distinct feeling that she wanted to ask me questions and hear more stories, but I was with friends and needed to leave. I felt familiarity between us, as if we had been together before in another time and space. Somewhere, somehow we'll meet again, and I'll have even more stories.

While inputting this story at the computer, I paused for a moment. The following screen saver came on, "Let the beauty we love be what we do."

Testing Me

Spirit often tests me by playing out one situation, then showing me the same event with a much different outcome. These are tests to see if I will listen and follow directions. A life could depend on my response.

I was in the first row of cars at a traffic light, turning left onto a very busy six-lane highway. I was heading for the airport on this bright, sunny day in June.

Three ten-year-old boys were waiting to cross the street on their bikes. Suddenly one of them darted from the curb as the light changed green for northbound traffic. This kid had angels with him that day. He was past the first car closest to the curb and right in front of the second and third cars that just accelerated, then slammed on their brakes. I saw the wide eyes and panic on the faces of the drivers of those two cars. Heart attack panic. I also saw the angels pushing the kid across the street like he was riding the wind. He rode another hundred feet after he arrived safely on the other side of the street. Then got off his bike and laid on the grass. He had to know that death was knocking at his door. His buddies were laughing. They didn't have a clue about the gift of grace their friend had just received.

Spirit then played out the whole scene again, as it could have happen. I saw him get hit, fly about fifteen feet in the air, and land in the middle of the intersection. I called 911 on my cell phone as I moved my van across the two lanes of traffic to my right to block anyone from running over him. Then I got out of the van and covered him with my travel comforter. I watched his soul leave the body and hover over him. I told him God was giving him the choice to stay on earth or pass on. I wrapped my right arm around his head and put my left hand on his chest to send God's love and energy into his body to keep him alive until EMS arrived. He talked to God. Once the paramedics came, I put a stone in his hand, got in my van, and continued my journey. No words were exchanged. I just disappeared. That's the way it's supposed to be. Come unexpected, leave undetected.

Two scenarios, different outcomes. One as it was. The other as it could have been. I stilled my mind, quieted my heart, and listened for the test results. "You passed. No more tests, just the real thing. God knows that you will act on the messages you receive without questioning or attaching to the results."

What happened may have been the jolt to give that young man his purpose and reason for living.

Angels in the Clouds

Have you ever seen angels in the clouds? They come in a variety of shapes and sizes just like people.

Sometimes the angel-clouds stretch across the sky and they're easy to spot. Find the head and the rest will follow. Sometimes they have a perfectly shaped head, body, wings, arms, feet, and face. Other times it's just the head with wings stretching out in opposite directions. There are far too many variations to list. You just need to scan the sky and feel the angels watching over you and sending love from above. They may even feel like departed friends and relatives. If you take your eyes off them, they will change shape and disappear...just like life. Savor each moment, for it's gone in the blink of an eye.

———————◆———————

Play or Pass

I was given the choice to be in service to God or pass up the opportunity after a conversation with two clerks at a religious bookstore. I stopped in the store to buy a birthday present for my mother and decided to talk with them about carrying this book you're reading now.

"Is it about Jesus?" one clerk asked me.

"No," I replied, "It's about my journey as an Earth Angel and the assignments I'm given."

"If it's not about Jesus, we can't carry it."

"Well I hear Voices and write what I hear. I'm a scribe," I explained.

The one clerk jerked straight up in the air and blurted out, "That's the work of the devil," and went scurrying off to the storage room. I was stunned. She knew nothing about me or my messages, yet made a judgment based on lack of knowledge.

After paying for the present, I received a message to pass on to the clerk behind the counter. I bent close to her and whispered, "I'll see you in heaven."

I got in my car and laughed. "What was that all about?" I asked Spirit.

"This is the kind of thing you may encounter after the book is published and you start talking. Many people lack your desire to serve with an open mind and heart. Let them know your messages are all good and from God. Anyone can do what you do if they have the desire to serve and listen to the still small voice of goodness and truth. You are being given the chance to stop doing God's work and return to a normal life, or continue on the journey to mastery of life. Just remember to speak your truth and know that the truth needs no defense."

There was never a doubt in my mind whether to play or pass on this phenomenal opportunity. This is the best job I could ever have in the whole world.

Lessons

Our marriage pots had been boiling
over for years, due to lack of
attention. Burners were crusted
and pots scorched. Meaty issues
stuck and burned. Until one day
the lids were removed, and the
marriage evaporated without
a trace.

Jane Ellis Conrad, October 1994

Simply Love

Love can be so complex, if sliced, diced, and overana-
lyzed. Or it can be joyful, peaceful, and full of bliss. Love takes
on many forms. It can be called a deep appreciation or the
ultimate in caring. But whatever you call it, Love isn't anything until you give it away.

It can be Love of God, Love of self, Love of family and
friends, Love of work, nature, beauty, and on and on.

To Love God is to know that you are His child. He will
always be wherever you are to comfort and protect you. Your
road may not always be easy, and that's His loving way of
confronting you with opportunities to make choices to learn
and grow. Like every good parent, he wants you to be happy,
maximize your talents, be the best you can be, and share yourself with others to make a positive difference.

The Love of self is when you strive to be the best you can be. Forgive yourself for mistakes you've made while learning life's sometimes painful lessons. It's giving yourself a break when others won't. It's deep appreciation for each day of life and making the most of each breath. It's giving yourself permission to be whoever and whatever you choose. It's joyful living and peace of mind.

The Love of friends is often easier than the Love of family. Some families start filling their garbage bags at birth. By the time the children reach adulthood, the dumpsters have been overflowing for years, and the landfill is filled to capacity. It's often hard to burn the garbage and render it ash to be rototilled under the earth so new crops can be planted and grow into beautiful beings. Blessed families treat each other with Love and Respect and live in Peace and Harmony.

Friends, on the other hand, are chosen. People hang around with others who share the same interests, philosophies, backgrounds, talents, abilities, passions, and so forth. Sometimes you just like the person, and don't really have much in common. In time, some of these attributes change, and you find new friends who share your current interests. Sometimes you keep in touch with the old friends, and other times they vaporize into the atmosphere never to be seen or heard from again.

The ultimate experience is sharing your life's journey with the love of your life, your best friend. The person who knows your inner workings…your strengths and weaknesses, good and bad, beauty and scars. The one who knows all about you, and Loves you anyway. If you pay attention, and are truly fortunate, you might even find your soulmate. It may start off with the meeting of eyes. A gentle touch. A kind word. A caring smile. A soft sigh. A wonderful friendship. Easy conversations. Long walks. Undercurrents of destiny. It's having the person walk through your mind when you're thinking about other things. The face...the scent...the sweet embrace. A yearning for a gentle touch when they're out of reach. The churning in the pit of the stomach when you're together.

Fortunate are those who have known true and lasting Love, for they have received God's greatest gift. Wise is he who has known Love and made the adjustments to make it last forever and a day. Blessed are the Loving Souls, for they shall have their heart's desires.

Ultimate Love Story

My Mom and I made our transitions on the same day: December 30, 1999. Hers was upward, mine inward. My energy field changed that day. It felt like God revved up my engine and started putting my affairs in order for the journey of a lifetime. I took the baton to continue what Mom and Dad started and will pass it on to whoever shares our passion for life and service when it's time for me to go.

Bill and Martha Ellis

Rather than mourn Mom's passing, celebrating her life seems more appropriate. She was totally dedicated to my father... the ultimate soulmate and support system. Together they dreamed big dreams. With action, those dreams became their reality. They were already a team before the players started coming two years later—my brother, sister, and I. We were wanted, loved, encouraged, supported, and given the best gifts any kids could get. They taught us about God by showing us how to live. We witnessed unconditional Love between them and everyone they touched. I'd call them Earth Angels—God's messengers sent to make the world a better place. They gave more than they took. Helped whomever, whenever, however, and wherever. Dispensed Random Acts of Kindness. They were prosperous both monetarily and spiritually. Living examples of whatever you give, you get back tenfold. Love and money flowed in and out. They never criticized, condemned, or complained. Just encouraged, cared, shared, laughed, and loved with all their hearts until death separated them on earth and then reunited them in heaven—Bill and Martha Ellis— together at last. Gone but not forgotten.

Let me share some things about them you may not know. Dad had a high school education yet was a registered architect in thirty-seven states. When he was forty-nine years old, and working for a large architectural firm, he joined forces with other dreamers and started an architectural/engineering firm. Pretty gutsy move when others in his position were thinking about retirement. Some say he was self-made. I called him a visionary with dreams bigger than life and the unstoppable desire to make a difference. He told his customers, "I just want to be your milkman—great products, reasonable prices, timely delivery, and friendly service." He treated everyone the same, from the elevator operator to the company president—a cheery smile, jokes, candy from his pocket or desk drawer, encouraging words, and a piece of his heart. He told me I was limitless.

Mom was the ultimate support system not only for Dad and our family but for friends, golfing buddies, Dad's clients, and any others fortunate to join her path. She was a talented golfer, writer, artist, seamstress, played the organ, and sang in the choir with Dad, plus was very competitive and excelled at everything she put her mind to. If born just one generation later, she would have been a "Superwoman" who balanced a family life with her executive position. Maybe she would have been the engineering half of Dad's company. They were passionate about work, life, having fun, and each other.

Together they walked hand-in-hand, singing in harmony *You Are My Sunshine, I Love You a Bushel and a Peck,* and other classics that run through my head and out of my mouth when I'm working, driving, or walking in the park. I hear them singing with me from heaven. My heart rejoices that they're finally together again. I recently told a friend, "I had the ultimate parents. I wish you could have met them." Her response brought tears to my eyes: "I did meet them... when I met you."

Before Death We Did Part

"Our marriage pots had been boiling over for years because of lack of attention. Burners were crusted and pots scorched. Meaty issues stuck and burned. Until one day the lids were removed, and the marriage evaporated without a trace." I wrote this one month before retiring from a twenty-four year marriage. I'm grateful for the lessons about love, sorrow, compassion, survival, boundaries, teamwork, expectations, commitment, and how to tell when the game is over.

How do people cope when their marriage dies before they do? I handled it the way so many others do. I sank into denial. We may not have the joyful loving relationship like Dad and Mom, but we have a nice home, loving animals, great vacations, wonderful friends. Is it worth giving up all these material things that we've spent half our lives acquiring for the unknown? Is this my last chance for love? Will anyone ever love and cherish me just for the kind, loving, honest, spiritual person I am?

It wasn't all bad. We liked to travel, play golf, go boating, and get together with friends. He was an avid reader. I was in constant motion always looking for something to do. I was a member of three local chambers of commerce, the Kiwanis Club, and two national women's organizations. On Saturday I volunteered to man a book cart at a nursing home then go to the animal shelter and clean out cages. Two smelly places, yet worthwhile jobs.

We lacked a common spiritual belief. Faith in something bigger than our egos. A God for all reasons and seasons. Our purpose for being on earth.

The marriage died so we could both live, be happy, and find out what lessons we are to learn in this lifetime.

How many other people are in this situation and feel helpless?

For years God had whispered, "You don't have to do this any more, Jane."

I thought I knew better. "But, God," I questioned, "what about my vows to love and cherish until death do us part?"

God responded, "When the marriage dies, you can part. You don't have to physically die to complete the contract. It's time to start your spiritual journey and find your purpose for being on earth."

I searched for a religion that made sense and could help me *now*...more psychology than dogma. A religion that would open my mind to think rather than condemn, belittle, berate, and tell me I'm unworthy and not going to heaven unless I believed what the minister said. I never did buy that bologna.

I'd still my heart and whisper, "How can I serve you, God, and be a better person?" I kept looking for God and searching for peace of mind and unconditional love. The Unity philosophy supplied the answers I was seeking. God is the center of the Universe and is in everything and everyone. The purpose of life is to be in God's service, to be the best you can be and help others. God is pure energy and has no gender. Religion is exterior—the words, spirituality is interior—the feelings. God is accessible to everyone—one on one—no middlemen are needed. This I believe. It doesn't matter to me if anyone believes the same way. They can get to God any way they want and it has nothing to do with me. I mind my own business and expect others to do the same.

Now I'm free to be and do whatever makes my heart sing. I write, paint, sing, dance, skip, and let my inner child come out to play. My Voices are with me all day, every day. We talk, laugh, sing, and smile a lot. They dictate poems, prose, and stories about my life. I am the scribe and they are the storytellers. One day they told me to buy colored pens, construction paper, and scissors. I cut out flowers and other forms, and they supplied the words. Thus the creation of a paper collage book, *Me...Thee...and People and Places Between*. The last picture in the book is blood draining from the bottom of a heart with the words "the bleeding has stopped, free to be me."

Survivors of Death

Tears filled his eyes. I was startled that the news about the new lump under my left armpit had caused an instant reaction. All I wanted to do was share information, not upset him. He knew about my cancer surgery in 1990 and must have thought it was back. His hug was so tight my breath was suspended for an instant. The audible prayer for my protection was straight from his heart.

Although he was a new friend, I wondered if my family would have the same reaction. My mother never talked to me about my cancer. Every time I started to, she would tell me about some stranger she golfed with the day before, or what the weather was like. I felt sadness at not having a mother to share my inner thoughts and feelings with. So I put them on the shelf in my mind where shattered dreams and disappointments reside. The "if only" shelf. Had she been through the same thing with her mother?

At that moment I realized that someone cared. And I had a responsibility not to share information casually that might harm others emotionally.

I've always believed that the ones who die are not the ones who suffer. Ideally they go to the light. Find God. Are greeted by relatives. Return to a healthy state of body, mind, and inner peace.

Then there are the ones left behind to grieve. Some people never get over the loss. Others remember the good times, celebrate the person's life, accept the change, and get on with their own lives.

In a way, each person has a responsibility to take care of themselves and live a healthy, productive life. Not just for themselves, but for the ones they love.

Sometimes family and friends pass on without having a chance to say goodbye. One day they leave for work and never return. I received that news one morning from my friend Karen's sister, Lynn. "There's been an accident. Larry was killed yesterday by a machine at work." My first reaction was disbelief. Then compassion for Karen and her family. What a loss. I closed my store, Recognition Express, and headed for Karen's house. There was no hesitation that being with her was more important than making name badges or signs. There were ten relatives and friends at the house when I arrived. All were in shock and somewhat dazed by what had happened. The details of the accident were sketchy.

This was a time for me to be silent, yet available to support the family any way I could. There was no hesitation when I was asked to read one of the lessons at the funeral mass. It was from Ecclesiastes 3:1–8: "All things have their season, and in their times all things pass under heaven. A time to be born, and a time to die…"

Instead of sending flowers, I took the letters of Larry's name, Laurence Arthur Green, and wrote about him, engraved the words on a plaque, and read it at the church service. Two other friends read scriptures. Then Larry's best friend since childhood, Bob, gave the eulogy. Such strength. He had just lost his best friend, yet got up in front of the audience of five hundred people and made us laugh with stories of their fun and mischief. They were like twins—full of life now parted in death.

After the service, eight of Larry's friends guided the casket from the church to the waiting hearse. It was so sad to see them standing helplessly in the parking lot unable to move, watching their friend's body being driven away. It was the last farewell.

When Karen and her family were standing outside the church, waiting for the cars to take them to the funeral luncheon, two giant dragonflies flew back and forth over their heads. After the family left, the dragonflies flew over the rest of the crowd for another fifteen or twenty minutes, then flew away. The dragonfly was the same symbol that came to me after my father passed in May, 1995. Every day that summer, I saw a dragonfly. They would land on me or my car antenna or drinking straw, or just fly in front of my face then disappear until the next day.

I asked Spirit why Larry left earth in the prime of his life and received this reply: "God called Larry home. His journey was swift and painless. He accomplished what he was sent to do by caring, sharing, laughing, and loving with all his heart. He touched a lot of people. Just imagine how peaceful this planet would be if everyone lived life so simply. But time will heal…and hearts will remember."

When I get to heaven, God is not going to care how many name badges or signs I've made, but rather how many hearts I've touched.

Smiling Down From Heaven
7/7/44 to 9/18/00

Lived life to the fullest.
Accessible to anyone in need.
Unconditional devotion and Love for his soulmate, Karen.
Ready to travel anytime, anywhere.
Enjoyed the four seasons—water to winter.
Natural with all those who crossed his path.
Craftsman with imagination and skill.
Everyone's friend, Bob's twin, Karen's "Darling."

Always ready to party.
Real witty, effervescent and endearing.
Terrific sense of humor and contagious laughter.
Happy heart and loving soul.
Unquestionable love for his family and friends.
Revved up and decorated his "Luv Truck."

Gourmet chef and barbecue king.
Road rally and white elephant organizer.
Enthusiastic choral director of Christmas carols and oldies.
Exercised and dieted when encouraged.
Now in God's hands…smiling and sending love from
    heaven.

Larry Touched So Many Hearts and Souls,
Now He's Just a Thought Away.

Football Played Out in Life

Life is like a football game. You're born in one end zone and work your way to the other end zone. Sometimes you catch a pass, have good blockage, and the distance is swift and painless.

Other times, you get knocked down, bloodied, and hurt real bad until you discover—Duh!— that football is a team effort. If you're the one with the ball, ask yourself, "Do I want to be the lone ranger riding alone with everyone trying to knock me off the horse *or* do I want to work with my team-mates and use their expertise so we can all succeed and win the game?" Is there really a choice? Alone—hurt. Together—success.

Sometimes you move ahead. Other times you get shoved back. Some players may even try to take your helmet with your head still in it.

There are yard markers, out of bounds, referees, huddles to strategize, and coaches screaming in your face with words of encouragement or something not so nice.

God is the scorekeeper and timekeeper in life and death. When God says your time is up, and the last breath passes through your lungs and lips, the game is over. The final time-out. Did your team win, tie, or loose? If you entered the field with any intention but winning, you missed the reason for playing.

When your game called *life* is over, what will the score be? Have you scored a touchdown? Got real close but never scored? Crashed and burned at the ten-yard line and made the decision not to get up and play any more? Your attitude determines your platitudes. In the end, what matters is not how many times you've fallen down, but how many times

THE JOYFUL JOURNEY OF AN EARTH ANGEL

you got up and marched toward the goal line. How many times you blocked the challenger to protect your teammates. The guts you had to follow your dreams when logic told you the tasks were too hard, the challenges too big, and the obstacles too great. It's the small victories not the big challenges that will get you to heaven.

What will your score be?

Be the best you can be and help everyone be their best—we are all on the same team in God's eyes.

————•◆•◆•————

Life's a Trip

When your soul is ready for another journey through life, God supplies the vehicle called a body. The body is assembled in the womb then drives down the birth canal into a vast sea of endless possibilities.

In the beginning, your trips are planned, fuel is supplied, vehicle is washed, plus preventive maintenance and repairs are done.

Eventually we are put in charge of our own vehicle. Some take care of it very well by eating, sleeping, and thinking well. Others choose to abuse it by smoking, drinking, eating lots of unhealthy food, working at jobs or relationships that drain and strain.

Some people set a destination, get the maps, fill up the tank, pack the bags, and do whatever action is needed to complete the journey and end up at the planned destination.

Other people have no destination. They head off in any direction not knowing where they will land. Often they blame others for their unhappiness and lack of success. If they don't know where they're going, how can they possibly know when they've arrived.

93

Some people also rely on others to take care of their health. That's like turning over control of your steering wheel and then blaming the chauffeur if your vehicle is not in good shape and breaks down.

If God gave you the vehicle of your choice at birth and told you to turn in the keys when you checked out of life, would you take care of it or trash it?

Your body *is* the vehicle. What will God say when you turn in the keys?

Turning "Can't" Into "Can"

I could hardly believe that I just told a new customer I couldn't do a job. He wanted me to engrave a tiny butler with a tray and the words "serving you" on a name badge along with a two-color logo, his name, and title. He faxed me the art, then called back.

"The butler is too small. I don't think I can do it," I said.

"Yes, you can!" he stated emphatically. I was stunned into silence. First, because I actually said I couldn't do something. My father taught me to use can't as a motivator not as a deterrent. Second, because this man was pretty adamant that it was going to be done, I compromised and said, "Okay, I'll try."

I put the artwork in my to-do pile, and forgot about it for a week. He called back. "Hi, this is Gordon. Did you get the badge done?"

Again I said, "The butler is too tiny. I don't think I can do it."

"Yes, you can!" he stated for the second time. Again, I agreed to try. Only this time I looked at the art every day for a week. Finally, I broke down and scanned it. I was excited.

Everything engraved crisp and clear, including the tiny buttons on the butler's shirt.

"Hi, Gordon. This is Jane. I got your badge done and it looks great."

"I knew you could do it," he said matter-of-factly. That was the beginning of a long, supportive friendship. If I ever lose my head and think "I can't," I dial Gordon and get the real answer. He's another Earth Angel and a phenomenal father.

Bird's-Eye View

It's interesting to see human lessons mirrored in the animal kingdom. I watched two sparrows hopping around on a brick wall surrounding my front porch. The male bird puffed up his feathers and vibrated with excitement. The female bird hopped over and pecked at him. He retreated then came within two feet of her and started the same gyrations. Again, she hopped over and started pecking at him. One time she pecked him so hard he fell off the wall onto the ground. After about twenty minutes she flew off to the north. He shook his feathers a few more times, looked around, and flew south.

I thought about human relationships. Some people will do anything to please their partner and all the other person can do is criticize. Then, if they're lucky, they fly off in opposite directions and find the people who do appreciate them.

Fly Away Home

Tears rushed to my eyes. Why now? Why tears for a baby bird when I hadn't felt these strong emotions for Princess Diana and Mother Teresa who just died? Was it sadness or helplessness?

I'd been cutting the grass when I noticed a fledgling sparrow hopping across the sidewalk through the grass and into the street pecking at morsels of food. One wing was dragging. It tried to fly, only to rise a few inches and land very close to its starting point.

Now the debate. Should I leave it alone or try to nurse it back to health? Can it defend itself against predators or am I responsible for protecting it?

"What do you want me to do, God?" I queried.

"Let your heart decide," came the reply.

My roommate helped me capture the nervous ball of squirming feathers. A trash recycling bin filled with fresh grass clippings, a plastic lid of water, birdseed, and a few ants became home. It hopped around and didn't try to escape. As long as it was eating and drinking, everything would be okay. Right?

"Please help me, God," I pleaded. Help me keep this bird safe from harm so it can heal and return to the wild.

I checked on it several times before going to bed. It was alert and lay very still as I stroked its back and softly told it everything would be okay. It had about a dozen dark brown feathers on its back, but most of its body was covered with fluffy gray baby feathers.

Morning came and I entered the garage with eagerness yet hesitancy. I wanted the box to be empty, and hoped the bird had fully recovered and flown out. Instead I found a cold, stiff, little brown form lying on its side. Sadness filled my heart as the tears rolled down my cheeks. I had failed.

Or had I?

Was it my fault the bird died? Should I have left it alone to fend for itself? Or had this little creature felt love from my quiet voice and gentle touch as it fought to live? And—what will I do next time? Will I turn my back and let nature take its course, or lend my helping hands?

Bug Lessons

Since my dad passed away in 1995, I have more awareness of all living things. Instead of squashing bugs, I observe them.

A fruit fly landed on my table at the restaurant and got stuck in a glob of ranch dressing on the place mat. I saw it struggle then give up when its wings became inoperable. I could have let it drown in the sea of white goo, but thought it would be a terrible death. How would that read on a tombstone? Took the wrong fork in the road and drowned in a sea of salad dressing.

I lowered my knife below the little critter and freed it from the quagmire. It kicked fast and furiously but couldn't flip over on its stomach. Out came the knife again to free it. It crawled away leaving a wet, white trail.

I reflected on the lesson I learned from another bug spotted on the floor in my doctor's office. First it crawled in one direction, then turned and continued the journey in the opposite direction, then turned again, and again, and again. That bug appeared to live a life that had no purpose. Will its life end with the stroke of a mop or the suction of a vacuum cleaner? Or will it set a goal to join its bug family?

How many people live like that bug? They wander through life with no agenda, purpose, goals, focus, or direction. Often they resent people who are successful and don't bother asking what steps they had to take or what sacrifices they had to endure to get there.

How many people wait to win the lotto called life and never know that their attitude *is* the ticket?

War or Roses

At a recent training class, I sat near the end of a long table next to my friend Katherine. On her other side sat Bud. When she left the room, I slid into her chair. Then she returned and sat in my chair.

About ten minutes later, she leaned over and whispered, "I don't like being on the end." To which I replied, "TS." Her eyes widened, and in a somber tone said, "FU." Seeing my shocked expression, she said, "Follow up." And I said, "Totally spiritual."

We laughed. Hugged and turned what could have been war into roses. I wonder how many wars have been waged when the outcome could have been so different.

Giving and Receiving

How many times have you heard, "It is better to give than to receive"? I've been on both sides and feel they are equally important.

THE JOYFUL JOURNEY OF AN EARTH ANGEL

My dad was Mr. Random Acts of Kindness. He was always giving, giving, giving. It was okay for a while, yet I never felt complete until I could give something back. Dad showed his love by giving me gifts, buying dinners and groceries, dispensing presents, buying cakes, and singing happy birthday when it wasn't anyone's birthday. He was a Master Giver. That is how he took care of his family, felt worth, and most of all showed love. It wasn't until he passed that I finally realized what he received every time someone said, "Thank you," smiled at his thoughtfulness, or acknowledged in some way that he had touched their heart. He was a heart massager. I showed my love not only with words, but by having him and Mom over for corned beef and cabbage, making a big pot of pea soup just for him, plus excelling at sports and work, and exhibiting the values they both taught me by being the best I could be.

I also learned that receiving is as important as giving. It's the circle of life. Sometimes you lead, sometimes you follow.

I also learned that it's better to give with no intention of getting anything back. But it does come back. And usually in greater abundance than I could ever imagine, in surprising ways and at unexpected times.

I also learned that it doesn't feel good to have someone give something and tell you what they expect back. Then I usually give them less than what they would have received if they had just given from their heart and let me give abundantly from mine. A big smile and kind loving words are excellent gifts.

One of the best gifts I have ever received came from my dear friend and Master Mind partner Barb. In 1996, she gave me the following piece for my birthday. I cried buckets over this act of kindness. She really knows me. She made an acrostic using the letters of my name Jane Ellis Conrad. Tears flowed when I saw the last letter "D—Devoted to those who cherish her." My entire essence was captured in six words. Thank you, Barb. I am blessed to call you my friend. I wish Dad and Mom were still here. This would have been a great gift to give them, too.

Otherwise Known As Daisy Jane

Joy is her middle name
Artistic with all that her hands touch
Naive and innocent in so many ways
Effervescent & endearing, she's just "too much

Earnest about her life's purpose
Love exudes from her very being
Loquacious, most times, but a good listener too
Imagination that doesn't stop seeing
Selfless to a fault

Creative when she doesn't even try
Original all the time
Natural with all those who cross her path
Refreshing like a breath of spring
Angelic in her human form
Devoted to those who cherish her

Happy 1996 Birthday to a very, very special friend!
Love, Peace and Joy!
Barbara Dych, 8/25/96

Comedy Castle?

What a relief to leave the smoke-filled, dimly lit room with amateur comedians spewing profanity. How this society is regressing from what comedy used to be. Somehow I can't picture Lucy telling Ricky to FU. Or Red Skeleton talking about his bedroom and bathroom habits. Or Sid Caesar and Imogene Coca talking about the size of their private parts. They knew all about comedy. The everyday humor. They could say so much with body language and facial expressions...and timing. I can still see Lucy and Ethel in the candy factory stuffing bonbons in their mouths, clothes, and anywhere else they could find room.

I wasn't the only one who found the raunchy humor tonight less than humorous. No one else was laughing. I went with two other friends to support one of our naturally funny friends who decided to try out her act. She used profanity, which took away from her natural humor. Kind of sad to think that she had to throw in the bad words to get onstage. The guy who got the most laughs made musical instrument sounds, did impersonations, and didn't swear. I wonder if the other noncomedians were paying attention.

Now I can say I've been there, done that, don't need to waste my money and time doing that again.

What lessons did I learn? It's good to support friends. It doesn't feel good to be bombarded with smut when I paid to hear comedy. It felt good to leave as soon as my friend performed. I was elated to walk to my car with friends, turn on the radio to WNIC's nice soothing music, and thank God I have choices.

Spiritual Path to Heaven

In the middle of editing the chapter, "Before Death We Did Part," I was interrupted by Spirit with the purpose of my journey and the final destination.

My purpose is to walk on a spiritual path and invite others to join me. Just keep walking, talking, and listening. Don't get off track or bogged down with details. The other people will join the journey and take care of the details. I just need to keep writing, writing, writing, speaking, speaking, learning, and *listening*. The destination is heaven. That's it!

The enlightened ones will be my teachers. The seekers of truth and light will be the protégés. Those who know the game of life is being played and want to join the team will buy my books, tapes, and be my audience. The messages are so simple:

1. Love versus fear
2. Forgiveness, love, mind your own business
3. Random Acts of Kindness
4. Caring, sharing, laughter, and love
5. Life is a football game—if you die with the score 0 to 0, you have to come back and play again
6. Stone of Endless Possibilities—a reminder that all you need is within your heart. You are limitless
7. Burning bowl to get rid of emotional garbage
8. Be the best you can be then help others do the same, if asked
9. Help, don't hinder

10. Release to peace

11. Religion is exterior—the words; spirituality is interior—the feelings

———— •◆•◆•◆•• ————

Now I Understand

From 1996 to 1999, I attended nine two-day motivational, company-sponsored events. Each time I had a partner and we joined two other twosomes to form a team to share thoughts and feelings. It is a spiritual and emotional tuneup I give myself every six months.

Homework is assigned on Saturday night to get in touch with goals and desires by creating dream books with photos clipped from magazines. Some people choose to work alone. I've found it more fun to work in a group where pictures can be shared. "Who needs a minivan, house, motor home, hunk-a burnin' love?" Several people have collected pictures of Oprah for me because my dream is to have my book chosen for Oprah's Book Club and be interviewed on her show. Achievement and success start with a dream, and I have a pile of Oprah heads.

In February, 2000 I volunteered to help with the training rather than be a participant. That's when my life changed, and I knew my spiritual life was alive and well.

While thumbing through magazines, the houses, cars, travel became less important than in the past. I put the magazines aside and opened the wooden chest where my memories are stored. There was a scraggly yellow bear puppet from a sixth-grade birthday party, some tiny wooden Japanese dolls from Uncle Andy, who is a missionary in Japan, and other doodads that only mean something to me. Then I looked through dozens of beautiful cards from friends: "You're a Real Angel...You're a Great Friend...Believe In Yourself... Knowing You Is a Blessing...." These are the pictures that make up my ninth dream book. There are no houses, cars, motor homes, or hunks-a burnin' love in this dream book...just feelings. No Oprah head either. If it's meant to be, God will let it happen! Until then, I'll just keep on dreaming, praying, listening, and releasing control of the outcome.

⋅⬩⬥⬩⋅

Love in a Music Box

Reid was in his early twenties when he came to my Recognition Express store, where I manufacture name badges, signs, plaques, awards, and banners, plus supply advertising specialties. He wanted to have a plate engraved for a music box that played "From This Moment." It was a three-month anniversary present for his wife, Jennifer.

As I read the words to be engraved, my heart sighed. This young man was a romantic, just like my dad. The paper he handed me read: "Jennifer, You are the greatest gift God ever gave me. You are my true love. Love, Reid."

He gave me a twenty dollar bill. I gave him change. After he left, I looked at the twenty dollars and sighed, thinking how lucky Jennifer was to be married to this kind, loving soul. Then the message came, "Give him the money back." I folded the twenty dollar bill and stuck it under a flap covering the music box works.

Two days later there was a message on my answering machine, "Hi, this is Reid. I would have paid for the engraving. My wife wasn't half as surprised as I was. Thanks."

I returned his call and related how much his love for Jennifer had touched my heart.

He said, "I've never had anyone do something so kind for me."

"I wanted you to go out to dinner on me," I said. "You were my Random Act of Kindness that day. Pass on the kindness to someone else." A few weeks later Reid brought his beloved Jennifer into my store to meet me. I felt their love for each other spilling over onto me. That was all the payment I needed. Precious moments...love in a music box.

New Soul

Same body, stronger and more determined energy. The shift was dramatic—and all because a friend saw the clutter in my life and told me I was out of integrity. That's all it took. That was on December 5, 2000. Within twenty-four hours, I had a completely new soul walk in and it was on a mission to declutter my life. This soul is more confident, articulate, focused on prosperity, and committed to success.

For six years I heard the message, "Clean up the clutter or you will not move forward." I listened but didn't act. My basement flooded four times and cleaned out some junk, but not nearly enough. Then I said a prayer, "God, how can I serve you full time?" That did it. The very next day the landlord called to say he was selling the house.

You might think that four floods and a move would get rid of all the unwanted clutter. Not quite—I just took it with me. My recognition manufacturing business moved from a 1600 square foot basement to an 850 square foot store. The change gave me a big, beautiful picture window that lets light stream in and the weather be noticed, but the clutter intensified.

I moved my dog, cat, and personal belongings from a three bedroom house to a one bedroom apartment. Seasonal equipment—like golf clubs, roller blades, skis, fold up chairs, coolers, and a tent—got crammed into either my conversion van or my very old, yet still reliable, rusty Pontiac Grand Am. They were my storage sheds on wheels.

Then, after my integrity challenge, I began to clear out the chaos. I emptied a half–garbage bag full of papers from the front seat, back seat, and trunk of my car. When the trash was gone and the car was washed and filled with gas, the energy became lighter.

Then I cleaned out the kitchen, bedroom closet, and bathroom before heading for my store on a "search and destroy clutter" mission. The more I discarded, the lighter I felt. What a difference. The energy was definitely better. I also cleaned out store receipts and bank slips I'd stuffed into my wallet along with crumpled dollar bills.

I guess it's true…the same messages and lessons keep repeating themselves until they are finally learned. Once the debris was cleared from my life, the energy flowed freely and easily along with prosperity.

Peace or Perish?

My new soul that arrived on December 5, 2000, is definitely bolder and more direct than my old one. Now I say and do things that would not have crossed my mind—or lips—before.

A few days after Christmas I headed to the mall for snow boots. I wanted to go to Sears. Three times an urgent message came, "Go to Penney's right now!" The parking lot was covered with mounds of snow; so the aisles were in disarray, caus-ing some inconvenience and frazzled nerves.

After finally parking, I walked toward Penney's and was stopped in my tracks by some nasty language coming from a distance behind me. Two men were screaming filthy, wash-their-mouths-out-with-soap obscenities at each other. They were in and out of their cars three times as I stood there watch-ing. All of a sudden I felt my body rushing toward them, my arms waving. I yelled, "Stop it. Just stop it. This is no way to act."

One man started to tell me his story. Then the other broke in with his version of this travesty. I looked at each of them and said, "Stop. Go home." One of them got in his car and drove away. I turned and walked toward the store. The sec-ond man pulled up to the stop sign and rolled down his window. "This is no way to start off the year," he shared. "No, it's not. It looks like you could use this," I said while dropping a Stone of Endless Possibilities and a pink card in his hand. "Make this a phenomenal year."

What did I just do? I screamed at two grown men, strang-ers. And they actually listened. The whole encounter made me laugh inside. Imagine what it looked like on the security parking lot monitor! The possibility that I could have been killed never entered my mind. And since I don't have chil-dren, the fact that they listened and obeyed totally baffled me. If this opportunity ever happens again, I know what to say, "If people do not stop fighting, we will perish. What's it going to be: PEACE or PERISH?"

ABOUT THE AUTHOR

Jane Ellis Conrad was raised in Grosse Pointe, Michigan, and resides in Rochester Hills, Michigan.

After a bout with cancer in 1990, she started five companies, plus published channeled music and art. Before that her professional background included positions in publishing, advertising, architecture, automotive, and robotics.

Her philosophy about life is simple: caring, sharing, laughter, and love. To help wherever she can. Listen to the silence. Perform Random Acts of Kindness. Make a difference.

She has been interviewed on television, radio, and newsprint for Random Acts of Kindness activities and nonsmoking issues.

APPENDIX

———•◆━◆•———

Contributions can be sent to:
>   The Edwarda O'Bara Fund
>   PO Box 693482
>   Miami, FL 33269-3482

Scholarship donations can be sent to:
>   Oprah's Angel Network
>   110 N. Carpenter Street
>   Chicago, IL 60607

The song "Random Acts of Kindness (Hearts Entwined Throughout the World)" is available from:
>   Kristen Hartnagel at (616) 874-4295
>   *Who Do You Want to Be?* (cassette)

Give the Gift of
Angels See Through Eagles' Eyes
to Your Friends and Colleagues

CHECK YOUR LEADING BOOKSTORE OR ORDER HERE

❑ **YES**, I want _____ copies of *Angels See Through Eagles' Eyes* at $14.95 each, plus $4 shipping per book (Michigan residents please add $.90 sales tax per book). Canadian orders must be accompanied by a postal money order in U.S. funds. Allow 15 days for delivery.

❑ **YES**, I am interested in having Jane Ellis Conrad speak or give a seminar to my company, association, school, or organization. Please send information.

My check or money order for $_____ is enclosed.
Please charge my: ❑Visa ❑MasterCard

Name_____

Organization _____

Address _____

City/State/Zip _____

Phone_____ Fax _____

E-mail _____

Card # _____

Exp. Date_____ Signature _____

Please make your check payable and return to:
Earth Angel Press
2899 East Big Beaver Road, #306 • Troy, MI 48083-2466
Phone: 248-299-5555
Fax your credit card order to: 248-299-5557
Email: earthangel@janeconrad.com
www.janeconrad.com

www.janeconrad.com